*Northwest Airlines
is proud to serve
Kevin Graham's
cuisine.*

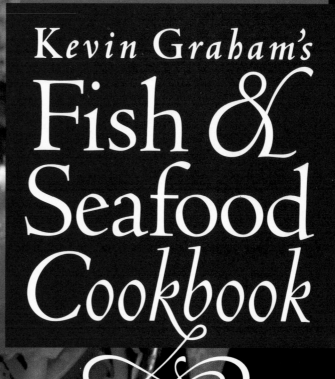

BODY CONSCIOUS CUISINE

Kevin Graham's
Fish &
Seafood
Cookbook

With Terri Landry

Photographs by Louis B. Wallach

Stewart, Tabori & Chang
New York

To Katie and Alexis

Published in 1993 by Stewart, Tabori & Chang, Inc.
575 Broadway, New York, New York 10012

Library of Congress Cataloging-in-Publication Data

Graham, Kevin.
    [Fish and seafood cookbook]
    Kevin Graham's fish and seafood cookbook :
body conscious cuisine / with Terri Landry ;
photographs by Louis B. Wallach.
        p.   cm.
    Includes index.
    ISBN 1-55670-265-5
    1. Cookery (Fish) 2. Cookery (Seafood) 3. Low-fat
diet—Recipes. I. Landry, Terri. II. Title. III. Title:
Fish and seafood cookbook.
TX747.G68   1993
641.6'92—dc20   93-17374
                                              CIP

Distributed in the U.S. by Workman Publishing
708 Broadway, New York, New York 10003

Distributed in Canada by Canadian Manda Group
P.O. Box 920, Station U, Toronto, Ontario M8Z 5P9

Distributed in all other territories (except Central
and South America) by Melia Publishing Services
P.O. Box 1639, Maidenhead, Berkshire SL6 6YZ, England

Central and South American accounts should contact
Export Sales Manager, Stewart, Tabori & Chang.

Printed in Japan
10 9 8 7 6 5 4 3 2 1

PAGE 1: *Roasted Cod with Leeks and Cream,*
recipe on page 56

PAGES 2–3: *Marinated Yellowfin Tuna,*
recipe on page 20

CONTENTS

Although I cook professionally, I like to think of myself as an artist as well as a chef. For me food is an outlet for expression, and my hope is that the recipes in this book reflect the joy I experience when cooking and eating fish and shellfish.

I coined the term Body Conscious about ten years ago to describe a philosophy of eating and exercise that I adopted in order to stabilize my weight as I treaded the path toward middle age. Even though I actually lost weight with my healthier lifestyle, Body Conscious is in no sense a "diet." In fact, I eat pretty much whatever I want, but I do so with common sense and appreciation of both the foods I am putting into my body and my body itself.

On the most basic level Body Conscious is a heightened awareness of how food affects us. I like to say that Body Conscious maximizes the minimum. I don't, for instance, avoid cream, butter, or other forms of fat, but I use these items with discretion. Most of the time I prefer to use flavored oils and even puréed potatoes as well as stocks, infusions, and simple reductions, all of which are healthier and, in my opinion, better tasting.

Tilapia with Citrus and Three Peppers, recipe on page 138

It has taken many years for me to arrive at this point in my cooking and eating philosophy, but I will be the first to admit that the evolution of Body Conscious is an ongoing process, and there is still much to accomplish.

I wasn't always interested in cooking and certainly nothing in my childhood indicated that I ever would be. The food of my upbringing was typical of Cheshire, a county in western England famous for its hard cheese and the grinning cat in Lewis Carroll's *Alice's Adventures in Wonderland,* but not for its haute cuisine. The fare was simple and hearty, made up of whatever fresh ingredients were available. As a child I had no desire whatsoever to help out in the kitchen. Like most young boys of my day, I opted instead to play cowboys and Indians outdoors.

My decision to become a chef was less a matter of what I wanted to be than what I didn't want to be: part of the establishment. It was the 1960s, and England was in the throes of a cultural revolution. I had no desire to enter any profession that I considered "respectable." I decided to become a chef because I thought it was suitably offbeat.

After two years of culinary training at Hollins College in

Manchester, I went to work at the Savoy Grill in London. There I was, still wet behind the ears, entering a world-class hotel kitchen. The noise, the heat, and the chaos were at once frightening and intriguing to me. I soon realized that I had joined (as a very, very junior member) a select and private corps.

In the nearly twenty years that have passed since then, I have had the opportunity to meet and man the culinary trenches with some extremely talented individuals in England, Europe, and the United States. In particular, I owe a great debt to a German chef named Klaus Ruliche. From this extraordinary man I learned not only how to properly handle the precious commodities of the kitchen, but also the values and work ethic necessary to meet the grueling demands of restaurant life.

I still apply daily many of the things I learned years ago from Klaus and my other mentors. The only difference is that I now avoid the heavy cream, butter, red meat, and other traditional ingredients that we depended on then but today acknowledge as being detrimental to our health when not used in moderation.

I began to change my approach to cooking—and myself in general—when I hit my early thirties. My waistline had begun to expand and I could no longer use the excuse that my pants were shrinking. My diet was improper: not the food per se, but rather the way it was prepared. In fact, my whole lifestyle was out of tune. I knew something had to change.

First I took stock of what I was as a human environment (out of shape) and visualized what I wanted to become (fit and healthy). I knew that food—in addition to eliminating hunger—soothes, comforts, and pleases. With that in mind, I started to explore a much simpler, lighter way of cooking that would still gratify the senses.

What I now call Body Conscious slowly took shape. Along with redefining my diet and eating habits, I gave up smoking, which heightened both my sensitivity to flavor and my sense of smell. I stopped drinking alcohol and I started to exercise. Wonder of wonders, my body responded and so did my attitude.

Like an artist, I began to assemble a new palette of seasonings and ingredients to enhance flavor and create complex mouth textures. Some of my "colors" came from memories of food I had eaten in the past and never forgotten, for instance, a steamed baby scallop with ginger dish that I had eaten at a Chinese restaurant in Manchester while I was still in school. As I traveled and tasted, other spaces on my palette were filled, most notably with the flavors of the cuisines of India and Japan. Nouvelle cuisine, a culinary Renaissance that focused on retaining the natural flavor of ingredients, also had a tremendous influence on my way of looking at food.

As I became Body Conscious I also became aware that we are all part of the same global ecosystem. I began to appreciate the symbiotic relationship we have with the world around us. Just as our bodies will not stay fit and healthy if we don't nurture them, our planet suffers when we abuse and neglect it. I now believe that the first step in environmental consciousness is for each one of us to take care of ourselves. In that way we can each take a small but significant step toward caring for the greater environment around us.

It is ironic that at a time when fish and shellfish consumption is at an all-time high, the natural harvest seems to be on the decline. A case in point is the giant bluefin tuna. Drawings of this giant fish on the caves of our prehistoric ancestors testify to its abundance, yet today the bluefin tuna is becoming more and more scarce. Increasingly, fish are found with deformities as a result of the toxins in our waters. And fishing boats continue to go out for one species and indiscriminately kill and dispose of the other fish they catch in the process. A single trawl over a reef can destroy in seconds an environment that took decades to build.

But the news is not all bad: The sea can replenish and heal itself. In order for this to happen, however, our global waters, like our bodies, have to be nurtured. Legislation must be enacted on an international level to protect our waters against pollution and overfishing and to protect endangered species against extinction by giving them the same endangered classification that certain mammals already have. We must reclaim the wetlands and take steps to prevent coastal erosion. And, most important, the general population must be made more conscious of the devastation occurring everyday and must work to prevent it.

In the meantime, aquaculture, the science of breeding fish in captivity, has begun to take up some of the slack and can continue to do so. Farming has already increased the supply and lowered the cost of shrimp, salmon, oysters, trout, catfish, tilapia, and striped bass. I imagine that the species of fish consumed over the next fifty years will be the ones that can be cultivated most easily, and perhaps this will give the natural underwater habitats time to begin healing.

USING THIS BOOK

Of all the vertebrates, fish are the most abundant. There are about four times as many known fish species as there are species of mammals. Because a fish's development, shape, and feeding habits are determined by its environment, the recipes in this book are organized according to aquatic habitat.

I begin offshore in the deepest waters of the sea, where commercial exploration is just beginning. From there I move closer to the shore, to the continental shelf, where the bulk of our fish and shellfish are harvested. Next I offer recipes for fish that live exclusively in fresh water, or spend part of their lives in fresh water and part in salt water. And finally I present recipes that utilize a combination of species that live in different habitats as well as the basic stocks and seasonings.

BUYING AND STORING FISH

When it comes to fish, quality depends on freshness. A properly processed fish can stay fresh for up to five days from the time it is pulled from the water. Improperly handled fish can spoil in just a few hours.

When selecting whole fish, look for clear, bright eyes and red, not gray, gills. The scales should be shiny and the flesh should feel firm and resilient. Fillets should be smooth and moist. Both whole fish and fillets should be displayed on ice and should smell clean rather than fishy. Whenever possible, avoid frozen fish or shellfish, and substitute an available fresh species instead.

At home, wrap fresh fish in plastic and store it in the coldest part of the refrigerator (32 to 38 degrees Fahrenheit) for up to 48 hours. Make sure the fish is not in direct contact with ice, as that will burn the delicate flesh.

COOKING FISH

Throughout this book, I've approached fish from the purest possible point of view, making every effort to retain natural flavors. I've taken readily available raw materials and transformed them into delicious meals with as little fuss as possible and a minimal amount of preparation.

Before preparation, rinse fish in cold water to remove any superficial bacteria. Cook fish and shellfish completely. Fish is done when the flesh turns opaque and it reaches an internal temperature of 140 degrees Fahrenheit. Since fish doesn't stop cooking the minute you remove it from the heat, it is always better to err on the underdone side rather than the overdone side. Also keep in mind that the fresher the fish, the quicker it will cook; if you want to test the accuracy of this claim, try the recipe for Blue Trout (page 133) in which freshly killed whole trout cook in a matter of minutes. Oysters, mussels, and clams should be steamed for four to six minutes, until they open.

From the time you take a fish out of the oven or off the stovetop or grill, it is going to release moisture and dehydrate, and it will continue to do so until it reaches the temperature of its environment. The secret to moist seafood is to get the product from its cooking medium to the table in the shortest amount of time possible. Cook fish at the last minute, then if you must hold it for a few minutes before serving, cover it with plastic wrap.

To protect the delicate flesh underneath and keep fish from drying out, leave the skin on during cooking. If you wish to remove the skin for serving, do so after the fish is cooked. There's nothing harmful about fish skin; it's nutritious and in most species (like salmon, bass, and cod) delicious.

Some people prefer to serve fish with the head and tail removed. It's far more pleasing for me, however, to see a fish—a trout, for instance—with its head on. It gives the fish character and identity.

Five easy and flexible methods for cooking fish are used throughout this book: sautéing or pan-frying over moderately high heat; poaching or simmering in stock on top of the stove; baking in a hot oven; broiling three to four inches from the heat source; and grilling over ashen coals. With few exceptions, no special equipment is needed. The bulk of the recipes simply require sharp knives, heavy stainless-steel frying pans and saucepans, nonreactive bowls, and, most important, a willingness to try new ideas.

While the recipes in this collection were created in a professional kitchen, all have been thoroughly tested in home kitchens as well. The dishes were chosen with the adventurous home cook in mind. It is my hope that they not only will stimulate your palate but also will inspire you to take care of your entire self—to become Body Conscious.

Roasted Weakfish with Beet Linguine, recipe on page 35

1

The Saltwater System

I *really enjoy the combination of fruit and fish. In this simple entrée the sweetness of oranges and the sharpness of radicchio are in delicious juxtaposition to the charred flavor of the seared tuna. The vibrant pinks, reds, and oranges in the dish are naturally pleasing, and remind me of sunshine.*

Cut the oranges into segments, removing any white pith, and place in a small bowl; reserve any juice that drains out of the segments.

In a large, heavy skillet, heat the oil to just below the smoking point. Season the tuna on both sides with salt and pepper. Sear the steaks in the hot oil for a minute or two on both sides. Do not overcook. Remove the tuna from the pan and drain on paper towels.

Divide the orange segments among four serving plates. Arrange a bed of Sautéed Radicchio and Endive on each plate. Place the tuna steaks on the lettuce and drizzle with any residual orange juice.

4 SERVINGS

4 blood oranges, peeled
¼ cup extra-virgin olive oil
4 skinless tuna steaks, about 8 ounces each
Salt and freshly ground black pepper
Sautéed Radicchio and Endive in Garlic
   and Mustard Vinaigrette
   (recipe follows)

❦

Wash the head of radicchio, removing any brown outer leaves. Drain and divide the head into eight pieces. Wash and remove any damaged leaves from the heads of endive. Drain and divide each head into four pieces. Place both lettuces in a large bowl.

In a small bowl, combine the oil, vinegar, garlic, mustard, salt, and pepper. Mix well.

Pour the vinaigrette over the lettuces and toss thoroughly. Let sit at room temperature for 20 minutes.

Bring a large heavy skillet up to smoking temperature; do not add any oil. Place the marinated radicchio and endive in the hot pan and toss rapidly for 20 to 30 seconds. Remove from the pan and serve warm.

SAUTÉED RADICCHIO AND ENDIVE IN GARLIC AND MUSTARD VINAIGRETTE

1 medium head radicchio
2 heads Belgian endive
¼ cup extra-virgin olive oil
2 tablespoons champagne vinegar
4 cloves garlic, crushed
¼ teaspoon dry mustard
Pinch of salt
Pinch of freshly ground black pepper

This traditional Italian dish typically features thinly sliced raw fillet of beef. I've reworked the recipe, substituting my favorite sashimi fish, yellowfin tuna.

4 SERVINGS

1 pound skinless yellowfin tuna fillet
1 tablespoon Oriental sesame oil
1 teaspoon soy sauce
2 ripe avocados
¼ cup loosely packed fresh dill sprigs
1 teaspoon grated fresh ginger
1 tablespoon cracked black pepper

Seal the tuna in plastic wrap and place in the freezer until firm but not frozen solid.

Combine the sesame oil and soy sauce in a small bowl and set aside.

Split the avocados lengthwise. Pull the halves apart and remove the pit. With a spoon, scoop the avocado flesh out of the peel, keeping each half intact. Cut into very thin slices.

On each serving plate, layer one quarter of the avocado slices, shingling, or overlapping, the slices. Arrange the dill sprigs on top of the avocado, then sprinkle with the grated ginger and the sesame oil–soy sauce mixture.

Remove the tuna from the freezer and, using a very sharp knife, slice it across the grain as thinly as possible. Spread the slices of tuna over the avocado. Sprinkle with cracked black pepper and serve immediately.

Sugar has many magical properties beyond sweetening. In this recipe I marinate the tuna in brown sugar before cooking it to firm up the flesh and lock in the moisture. I like to use Demerara sugar, a soft, less-refined, molasses-flavored sugar, but any light brown sugar will have the same effect. Although the fish is well rinsed following marination, enough of the sugar is absorbed to form a sweet crust during cooking. I discovered quite by accident that the heat of cooked fish causes thinly shaved bonito flakes to move, or "dance." It's an amusing presentation that adds a festive note to any gathering.

4 SERVINGS

¼ cup light brown sugar (preferably West Indian Demerara brown sugar), divided
½ teaspoon crushed red pepper
4 skinless tuna steaks, about 8 ounces each
2 tablespoons Red Pepper Oil (see Index)
¼ cup chopped fresh ginger
2 cups Chicken Stock (see Index)
4 ounces bean sprouts, washed and dried
1 teaspoon bonito flakes (dried tuna, available at Asian markets)
Salt and freshly ground black pepper
1 small red bell pepper, seeded and cut into thin rings, for garnish

In a small bowl, combine 2 tablespoons of the brown sugar and the crushed red pepper. Place the tuna steaks in a shallow dish and sprinkle with the brown sugar mixture. Cover and marinate for 1 hour in the refrigerator.

Rinse the steaks under cold running water and pat dry with paper towels. Season the tuna on both sides with salt and pepper.

Heat the red pepper oil in a large skillet until it begins to sizzle. Sear the tuna in the hot oil for 1 minute per side. Remove from the pan and keep warm.

Pour off any oil remaining in the skillet, then add the remaining brown sugar. Cook over low heat until the sugar dissolves and caramelizes. Stir in the ginger and chicken stock; reduce by half over high heat. Lower the heat and keep the stock hot until serving.

Mound the bean sprouts in the center of four ovenproof plates. Place the seared tuna on the sprouts and sprinkle with the bonito flakes. Pour 1 tablespoon of the ginger stock around each piece of tuna and garnish with the bell pepper rings. Serve immediately.

Yellowfin tuna is highly prized in Japan, where it is eaten raw. The tuna in this modified sashimi is seared briefly before it makes its way to the table.

4 SERVINGS AS AN ENTRÉE, 8 AS A SIDE DISH

4 skinless yellowfin tuna steaks, about
    8 ounces each
2 cloves garlic, crushed
Juice of 2 limes
1 jalapeño pepper, seeded and finely
    julienned
1 teaspoon finely julienned fresh ginger
2 cups mung bean sprouts
½ cup peeled and finely julienned
    cantaloupe

Before cooking the tuna, fill a medium bowl with about 4 cups of cold water and 2 cups of ice.

Preheat a grill or broiler to very hot. Grill or broil the tuna steaks for 30 seconds per side. Remove from the heat and plunge into the ice water. When chilled, drain the steaks and pat dry with paper towels.

With a very sharp knife, finely julienne the steaks, cutting across the grain. Place the julienned tuna in a medium bowl and add the garlic, lime juice, jalapeño, and ginger. Mix thoroughly and let sit at room temperature for 20 minutes.

In another medium bowl, toss the sprouts and cantaloupe. Serve the tuna mixture on a bed of sprouts and cantaloupe as an entrée or side dish.

Tilefish live 45 to 170 fathoms below, on the bottom of the northwest Atlantic. This species thrives in temperatures around 50 degrees Fahrenheit. In fact, water temperature is so important to this colorful fish that a shift of a cold-water current in 1882 killed millions of tilefish north of Delaware Bay and nearly wiped out the species.

4 SERVINGS

4 tilefish fillets, with skin, about 6 ounces
    each
2 tablespoons canola or extra-virgin
    olive oil
8 shallots, peeled
1 teaspoon sugar
¼ cup dry white wine
4 ounces (½ cup) blackberries
Salt and freshly ground black pepper

Preheat the oven to 375 degrees F.

Score the fillets on the skin side and season both sides with salt and pepper.

Heat the oil in a heavy ovenproof skillet until almost smoking. Place the fillets, skin side down, in the hot oil and cook until crisp, 1 to 2 minutes. Turn and cook the flesh side for 1 minute, then transfer to a baking sheet. Bake for 3 to 5 minutes, until the fillets are firm to the touch; remove from the oven and keep warm.

To the skillet, add the shallots and sauté until lightly browned on all sides. Sprinkle with the sugar, then place the skillet in the oven for 10 minutes. Return the pan to the stove and add the wine. Reduce by half over high heat. Stir in the blackberries and cook for a couple of minutes over low heat, until the berries start to swell.

Pool the shallots, warm blackberries, and sauce in the center of each of four serving plates. Place a tilefish fillet, skin side up, alongside the pool of sauce.

❦ OPAH WITH RED BANANA SCALES DUSTED WITH CINNAMON ❦

Since opah, also known as moonfish, is a tropical species, I decided to pair it with other tropical ingredients. I particularly like the visual contrast of the pink meat of the fish, the creamy pink of the banana, the deep red of the cinnamon, and the white flesh of the litchi fruit. Red bananas are much sweeter and more intensely flavored than the cultivated yellow variety: if red bananas are unavailable, substitute mango or papaya.

Preheat the oven to 400 degrees F.

In a small bowl, combine the cinnamon and coconut.

Season the opah fillets on both sides with salt and pepper.

In a heavy ovenproof skillet, heat the oil to almost smoking. Sear the fillets briefly, about 1 minute on each side, then remove from the pan and dust with the combined cinnamon and coconut.

Return the opah to the skillet. Arrange a sliced banana on top of each fillet, overlapping the slices to resemble fish scales. Place the skillet in the hot oven for 7 to 10 minutes. To test for doneness, press the thickest part of the fillet with a finger. The fillets are fully cooked when the juices are clear rather than milky. When the fillets are done, remove them and drain on paper towels. Keep warm.

Toss the litchis in the lime juice and serve with the warm opah fillets.

4 SERVINGS

1 teaspoon ground cinnamon
2 tablespoons ground coconut
4 opah fillets, with skin, about 8 ounces each
2 tablespoons canola oil
4 ripe red bananas, peeled and thinly sliced (keep each banana together as you slice)
1 pound fresh litchis, peeled, halved, and pitted
Juice of 1 lime
Salt and freshly ground black pepper

Marlin deteriorates more quickly once out of the water than its cousin the swordfish. For this reason, marlin were previously fished in large part for sport rather than consumption. They can weigh as much as a ton and all deep-sea fishermen and -women worth their salt sport marlin among their collections. Today, modern fishing boats with processing equipment on board make it possible to get marlin to the table while still fresh.

I particularly like smoked marlin. Because of the tightness of its flesh, you don't have to subject marlin to lengthy smoking to impart flavor.

4 SERVINGS

1 medium zucchini
1 medium yellow squash
Extra-virgin olive oil, for brushing
1 teaspoon finely chopped fresh thyme
 leaves
¼ cup balsamic vinegar
4 skinless marlin steaks, about 10 ounces
 each
Salt and freshly ground black pepper
Oak chips, soaked in water for 20 minutes
Thyme sprigs, for garnish (optional)

Heat charcoal until ashen in a covered outdoor barbecue.

Trim the ends of the zucchini and yellow squash and slice lengthwise into ribbons the approximate thickness of a penny. Brush the slices on both sides with olive oil.

Place the squash slices on the grill a few at a time; do not crowd. Cook the slices briefly, about 1 minute, until scored with grill marks. Turn the slices and score the other side, then remove from the grill and place in a shallow dish or rimmed baking sheet. When all the squash slices have been grilled, season with the thyme and salt and pepper, and sprinkle with the vinegar. Set aside.

Season the marlin steaks with salt and pepper on both sides. Make sure the coals are still white hot, then sprinkle with a handful of the soaked oak chips.

Brush the grill rack with oil and place the marlin steaks on the center of the grill; close the barbecue. Cook for 2 minutes, then remove the cover to release the smoke. Continue to cook the steaks about 5 minutes per side, until firm to the touch. Let rest for several minutes before serving.

Arrange the zucchini and squash ribbons in the shape of a wreath around the edges of four serving plates, folding one end of each piece of zucchini or squash under itself and overlapping each piece with the next piece (see photo). Set the marlin steaks in the center of the wreaths, garnish with thyme sprigs, if desired, and serve warm.

In the late 1970s, while traveling in the Caribbean, I happened to observe some island natives paring mangos by making incisions all over the globe, almost to the depth of the pit, then curling the fruit back. I had all but forgotten the unusual technique until presented wth the challenge of changing the appearance of shark flesh. Given the dense texture of the meat, the islanders' method was a natural. Here deep incisions make the shark flesh look similar to the petal-like tentacles of a sea anemone; the tabbouleh suggests the sand on the ocean floor where the gentle creature rests.

Arrange the mako steaks in a shallow dish and add the milk. Cover and refrigerate for 2 hours.

Combine the remaining ingredients through the olive oil in a blender or food processor and blend to a smooth paste. Set the mixture aside.

Preheat the broiler.

Drain the mako and pat dry. With a sharp knife, score each steak with deep crisscross lines; do not cut all the way through the flesh.

Place the steaks on a baking sheet and rub the anchovy paste into the incisions. Broil for 10 minutes.

Serve broiled mako with tabbouleh on the side. Garnish with the fresh fennel or dill.

4 SERVINGS

5 skinless mako steaks, about 8 ounces each
4 cups milk
8 anchovy fillets, drained
1 teaspoon finely chopped fresh parsley
Pinch of fresh rosemary
Pinch of fresh thyme
Pinch of fresh basil
Pinch of fresh marjoram
Pinch of fresh tarragon
Pinch of curry powder
Pinch of black pepper
Pinch of white pepper
1 clove garlic, finely chopped
5 pitted black olives
1 tablespoon extra-virgin olive oil
Tabbouleh (recipe follows)
Fresh fennel or dill sprigs, for garnish

❦

Place the bulgur in a medium bowl and add cold water to cover. Soak for 5 to 10 minutes, then drain in a colander lined with several thicknesses of cheesecloth. Wrap the bulgur in the cheesecloth and squeeze until completely dry.

Place the bulgur in a deep bowl and add the tomatoes, parsley, scallions, lemon juice, and salt. Toss gently with a fork, then let sit for 2 to 3 hours.

Before serving, fold in the mint and olive oil. Serve at room temperature.

TABBOULEH

½ cup fine (#1) bulgur
3 ripe tomatoes, peeled, seeded, and finely chopped
1 cup finely chopped fresh flat-leaf parsley
1 cup finely chopped scallions
⅓ cup lemon juice
1 teaspoon salt
3 tablespoons finely chopped fresh mint leaves
⅓ cup extra-virgin olive oil

Because of its meaty flesh, swordfish is sometimes compared to veal. I prefer not to liken fish to meat, however, since it strikes close to the hackneyed claim that everything from rabbit to turtle tastes like chicken. The dense texture of swordfish makes it perfect for barbecuing, and I recommend serving juicy grilled steaks with a crisp, refreshing salsa.

4 SERVINGS

4 skinless swordfish steaks, about
   10 ounces each
2 cups cold milk
Juice of 1 lemon
Dash of Worcestershire sauce
1 teaspoon Hungarian paprika
Extra-virgin olive oil, for brushing
Apple Salsa (recipe follows)

Rinse the swordfish steaks under cold running water, then place in a shallow dish with the milk. Soak for 1 hour in the refrigerator; this process will draw out any blood.

In a small bowl, combine the lemon juice, Worcestershire sauce, and paprika. Remove the steaks from the milk and rinse under cold running water again. Coat the swordfish on both sides with the lemon juice mixture and set aside while preparing the barbecue grill.

In an outdoor grill, heat charcoal until ashen. Oil the grill rack and place the swordfish steaks in the center of the hot grill. Cook just until scored with grill marks, 1 to 1½ minutes. Turn and score the other side, then move the steaks to the side of the grill or raise the grill rack and continue to cook for approximately 5 minutes, until the meat of the fish is opaque and firm to the touch.

Remove the steaks from the grill and let rest for 5 minutes before serving. Place on dinner plates and nap chilled Apple Salsa over one corner of the fish.

❦

APPLE SALSA

2 Granny Smith apples, cored and finely
   diced (do not peel)
½ green bell pepper, seeded and finely diced
½ red bell pepper, seeded and finely diced
2 jalapeño peppers, seeded and finely chopped
½ medium onion, finely chopped
2 tablespoons fresh cilantro, finely chopped
¼ European cucumber, peeled, seeded,
   and finely chopped
2 cloves garlic, finely chopped
Juice of 3 limes
3 tablespoons extra-virgin olive oil
Salt and freshly ground black pepper

Combine all the ingredients in a large bowl. Mix thoroughly and chill for 2 hours in the refrigerator before serving.

I like to pair grilled tuna with Japanese red rice, an unpolished rice with a red-tinged husk. The slightly sweet, short-grained rice has a nutty flavor that suits the distinctive taste and firm, meaty texture of the highly prized fish. If red rice is unavailable, substitute Italian arborio rice or short-grain brown rice. Avoid using a commercial polished rice.

If there is a lot of blood, which is sometimes the case with tuna, marlin, mackerel, and herring, soak the fish in milk prior to cooking. This technique, borrowed from the preparation of calves' liver, eliminates the strong, fishy flavor that some people find objectionable.

Place the rice in a medium bowl and cover with cold water. Let sit for 20 minutes, then drain in a fine sieve.

Preheat the oven to 375 degrees F.

Heat the oil in a heavy ovenproof skillet. Add the chopped shallot and sauté until clear. Stir in the rice and bay leaf. Sauté for 1 minute, then add the chicken stock. Cover the pan and transfer to the hot oven. Roast for 15 minutes; do not remove the lid or stir during cooking. Remove the pan from the heat and keep it covered.

Light a grill or preheat the broiler.

Season the tuna steaks on both sides with salt and pepper. Sprinkle with the lemon juice and grill or broil about 1½ minutes per side, until the steaks are scored with grill marks and the flesh loses its translucency; cooking time will vary depending on the heat of the grill.

Just before serving, fold the mint and vinegar into the rice. Shape into quenelles, or tablespoon-size ovals, and serve alongside the grilled tuna.

4 SERVINGS

1 cup red rice (available at Asian markets)
2 tablespoons peanut oil
1 shallot, finely chopped
1 bay leaf
¾ cup Chicken Stock (see Index)
8 skinless tuna steaks, about 3 ounces each
Juice of 1 lemon
1 loosely packed cup fresh mint leaves
½ teaspoon vinegar
Salt and freshly ground black pepper

Though virtually unknown to the modern cook, chlorophylls—the pure essences of vegetables—have flavored dishes since the turn of the century, when the chefs of the Grand Cuisine of Europe concentrated on the complete and total utilization of each ingredient. I first encountered chlorophylls while working in classical European kitchens, where they were used primarily to produce vegetable glazes for cold dishes. The technique can be used with any green vegetable or herb, such as asparagus or parsley. Here the tradition is revived in a recipe that features monkfish, also known as "poor man's lobster," with a cilantro chlorophyll.

4 SERVINGS

½ cup loosely packed fresh cilantro leaves
1 teaspoon sugar
1 tablespoon dry vermouth
4 ripe bananas
¼ cup plus 2 teaspoons light vegetable oil
1 cup cooked basmati rice (if using the
    recipe on page 99, omit the turmeric)
12 skinless medallions of monkfish, about
    2 ounces each
All-purpose flour, for dusting
Salt and freshly ground black pepper
Banana slices and parsley, for garnish
    (optional)

To make the chlorophyll, place the cilantro, sugar, and vermouth in a blender. Blend for 2 minutes or until the consistency resembles green soup. Strain through a fine sieve into a bowl. Cover and refrigerate.

Begin the timbales by peeling the bananas and slicing each one lengthwise into three pieces. Brush the middle slice of each banana with vegetable oil and cook in a sauté pan until lightly browned on one side. Remove from the pan and let cool. Curl each slice, browned side facing out, around the inside of a 2-inch-by-1-inch timbale mold. Repeat with three more molds.

Chop the remaining banana slices, toss in a teaspoon of the vegetable oil, and fold into the rice. Press the rice mixture into the timbale molds.

To prepare the monkfish, remove the white membrane and pound the fish gently. Dust the medallions with flour and season with salt and pepper.

In a large, heavy skillet, heat ¼ cup vegetable oil over moderately high heat. When hot, add the medallions and sauté for 1 to 2 minute per side until fully cooked. Remove and drain on paper towels.

Invert the banana timbales onto the side of four serving plates and unmold. Brush the monkfish with the cilantro chlorophyll and arrange 3 medallions on each plate. If desired, garnish with slices of banana and parsley.

Since the flesh of halibut tends to be dry, it is important that it be under- rather than overcooked, and that the cooking medium introduce moisture back into the flesh. For this reason I often serve halibut in a sauce. Here I chose a light cream sauce perfumed with pink peppercorns.

4 SERVINGS

2 tablespoons unsalted butter
2 cups (about 2½ ribs) finely julienned celery
¼ cup finely julienned shallots (onion may be substituted)
1 bay leaf
4 halibut steaks, with skin, about 6 ounces each
2 cups Fish Stock (see Index)
¼ cup dry white wine
2 tablespoons heavy cream
½ teaspoon crushed pink peppercorns
Salt and freshly ground white pepper
Dried lemon peel (instructions follow), for garnish
Celery leaves, for garnish

Preheat the oven to 375 degrees F.

In an ovenproof poaching pan or large ovenproof skillet, melt the butter. When it starts to bubble, add the celery, shallots, and bay leaf. Cook over medium heat until the vegetables are translucent. Place the halibut steaks on top of the celery mixture, then add the fish stock and wine. Cover the pan with parchment paper and bring to a rolling boil. Transfer to the hot oven for 8 to 10 minutes.

Remove the fish from the pan and keep warm. Place the stock and celery mixture in a blender; remove and discard the bay leaf. Blend the mixture to a purée, then pass through a fine sieve into a small saucepan. Cook over high heat until the amount of liquid is reduced by about a third, approximately 5 minutes. Add the heavy cream, strain the mixture into another small saucepan, then stir in the pink peppercorns. Adjust the seasoning with salt and white pepper to taste. Keep warm until serving.

Gently peel the skin from the halibut by grasping the skin at one corner and pulling diagonally across the steak to the other corner.

Spoon a little of the sauce in the center of four serving plates and top with a piece of halibut. Nap sauce on one corner of each steak and sprinkle with dried lemon peel. Garnish with celery leaves and serve.

❦

DRIED LEMON PEEL

Using a very sharp knife, peel the yellow part of the lemon rind. Place on a clean cloth or paper towels and let dry for 5 to 6 hours in a warm room, turning periodically. Chop very fine and store in an airtight container.

I like to play with contrasts. In this recipe, I have paired turbot, one of the most expensive fishes and a personal favorite, with lentils, one of the most economical legumes. The stark whiteness of the turbot against the green of the lentils makes a most striking presentation. It is a simple, healthy dish in which the delicate flavor of the fish shines.

In a small bowl, combine the wine, oil, shallot, and pepper. Stir until well combined, then rub the mixture over the white meat of the turbot. Place the fish in a shallow dish, cover, and marinate in the refrigerator for 2 hours.

Light a grill or preheat the broiler.

If grilling, place the fillets, flesh side down, on the hot grill rack. When scored, turn the fillets and move them to the outer edges of the grill until done, about 3 minutes.

If broiling, place the fillets, flesh side up, on a baking sheet and position the baking sheet as close to the heat source as possible. Broil the fillets for several minutes until flaky and opaque, watching carefully to avoid burning the fish. Let the turbot rest for a minute, then serve with Curried Lentils and warm pita bread on the side.

4 SERVINGS

¼ cup dry white wine
2 tablespoons extra-virgin olive oil
1 shallot, finely chopped
Pinch of freshly ground black pepper
4 turbot fillets, with skin, about 8 ounces
   each
Curried Lentils (recipe follows)
Pita bread

❦

Rinse and pick over the lentils for small stones, then set aside.

Heat the oil in a large sauté pan over moderately high heat. Add the onion, garlic, and ginger. Cook over moderately high heat until the onion is transparent, then add the spices. Sauté for 2 minutes, then stir in the lentils. Pour in 4 cups chicken stock, cover, and simmer until the lentils are tender, about 45 minutes. Stir occasionally and add more stock if the lentils start to dry out.

Before serving, adjust the seasoning with salt and pepper and remove the bay leaf.

CURRIED LENTILS

1 cup dry lentils
2 tablespoons canola oil
1 cup diced onion
2 cloves garlic, finely chopped
1 tablespoon finely chopped fresh ginger
1 tablespoon chili powder
1 teaspoon ground cumin
1 teaspoon ground cardamom
½ teaspoon ground turmeric
½ teaspoon cayenne pepper
1 teaspoon curry powder
½ teaspoon ground mace
½ teaspoon allspice
1 bay leaf
4 or more cups Chicken Stock (see Index)
Salt and freshly ground white pepper

Although lemonfish are widespread in the Gulf of Mexico and warm waters worldwide, they are not yet commercially significant. Too bad, because the large fish really has a delicious flavor. This is another species with several regional names; look for cobia, ling, or crabeater—no doubt a reference to its diet of crustaceans and small fish. If lemonfish are unavailable, substitute fillets of any flaky fish, such as snapper, grouper, or cod. Initially, I roasted whole snapper coated with pesto and discovered that the pesto formed a thick crust on the white flesh of the fish. I now use the technique in the preparation of lemonfish and other fish, such as tilapia. As the pesto crust is forming, any excess oils from the fish drain out of the fish and into the cooking vessel.

Preheat the oven to 450 degrees F. In a blender or food processor, combine the olive oil, pine nuts, basil, garlic, Parmesan, and Romano. Blend on high speed to a smooth paste.

Season the fish on both sides with salt and pepper, and spread with the basil pesto. Place the fish on a rimmed baking sheet and roast for 5 minutes, then reduce the temperature to 350 degrees F. and roast an additional 7 to 10 minutes until the fish is flaky and opaque.

Remove the lemonfish from the oven and let rest for 5 minutes before dividing into four portions. Serve with Angel Hair Pasta and Lemon on the side.

❦

In a large pot, bring 1 gallon of salted water to a boil. Cook the pasta in the boiling water for 2 to 3 minutes, stirring continuously. When the pasta is tender, drain it in a colander, then plunge the colander into ice water to cool off the pasta. Lift the colander from the ice water and drain as much water as possible from the pasta.

In a large bowl, toss the pasta with the lemon juice, olive oil, and parsley. Sprinkle with the Body Conscious Pepper and serve.

4 SERVINGS

½ cup extra-virgin olive oil
1 tablespoon pine nuts (roasted according
    to the instructions on page 123)
1 tablespoon chopped fresh basil leaves
1 clove garlic
1 tablespoon freshly grated Parmesan cheese
1 tablespoon freshly grated Romano cheese
2 pounds lemonfish fillet, with skin
Salt and freshly ground black pepper
Angel Hair Pasta and Lemon
    (recipe follows)

ANGEL HAIR PASTA AND LEMON

12 ounces dried angel hair pasta
Juice of 1 lemon
2 tablespoons extra-virgin olive oil
1 tablespoon chopped fresh parsley
½ teaspoon Body Conscious Pepper
    (see Index)

This member of the needlefish family can be found in the waters of the northeastern Atlantic, the Mediterranean, and Australia. As a matter of fact, this recipe evolved during a trip Down Under. The garfish I lunched on while venturing from Melbourne to Adelaide were cooked on a camp stove and were eaten with tangelos, the only fresh fruit available in the market that winter day. Garfish have extremely soft flesh and must be handled gently during preparation. If necessary, you can substitute sardines for the garfish and oranges for the tangelos.

4 SERVINGS

4 tangelos
16 baby garfish
Extra-virgin olive oil, for brushing
2 tablespoons sugar
2 tablespoons unsalted butter
½ cup dry white wine
1 teaspoon arrowroot
1 tablespoon dry vermouth
1 teaspoon finely chopped fresh chervil
   leaves, plus whole leaves for garnish
Salt and freshly ground black pepper

Prepare a grill or preheat the broiler.

Using a citrus zester or paring knife, remove the zest from the tangelos. Finely chop the zest and set aside. Peel and segment the fruit. Place the segments in a bowl and reserve.

Wash the garfish, then clean and gut the fish with a sharp knife. Scrape off the scales and make crisscross incisions down the length of both sides of each fish. Rinse the fish and pat dry with paper towels.

Season the garfish with salt and pepper, then brush with oil. Grill or broil the fish for 1 minute on each side. Remove from the heat and keep warm.

Place the sugar in a small, heavy saucepan and cook over medium heat, stirring constantly, until it melts and caramelizes; do not allow the sugar to burn.

Add the butter to the caramelized sugar and mix well. When the butter is fully incorporated, add the zest, white wine, and any juice from the tangelos.

Combine the arrowroot and vermouth in a small bowl. Gradually add the arrowroot mixture to the saucepan, stirring constantly, until the sauce is thick enough to coat the back of a spoon. Strain the sauce through a fine sieve into a clean saucepan and add the chervil.

To serve, spoon the sauce onto the base of four serving plates. Fan four garfish on each plate and garnish with the tangelo segments and whole fresh chervil leaves.

The weakfish is thus named because it has a mouth structure so delicate, or weak, that it tears easily when hooked. The popular game fish belongs to the croaker family, whose members drum, hum, croak, purr, or otherwise produce sound. Some experts now believe that the source of the deadly Siren Song of Greek mythology was none other than the weakfish, which swims the Mediterranean and other seas. Trout or salmon can be used in place of weakfish in this recipe.

Place the unpeeled beets in a large pot and add cold water almost to cover. Bring the water to a boil and place a lid on the pan. Cook over moderately high heat for 30 to 40 minutes, until tender; older beets may take longer to cook. Drain the beets and let cool.

To make the beet linguine, use a commercial vegetable slicer to slice the beets into long, flat "noodles." Place a beet on the spindle and turn the handle; the blades will cut continuous strings of beets. Alternatively, finely julienne the beets with a sharp knife or a food processor. Place the beets in a large bowl and set aside.

In a small saucepan, warm the vinegar. Add the brown sugar and cook over low heat, stirring, until the sugar dissolves. Remove from the heat and let cool.

Fold the scallions and the vinegar mixture into the beets and let sit at room temperature for 1 hour.

In a small bowl, combine the cracked black pepper and cilantro. Set the mixture aside while preparing the fish.

Preheat the oven to 400 degrees F. Rinse the weakfish thoroughly, then season with salt and pepper. Rub the fish inside and out with the pepper oil and place on a baking sheet. Bake in the hot oven until the flesh is firm, about 15 minutes. Remove the fish from the oven and let rest for 5 minutes. While the fish is warm, remove the skin by pulling it gently from the head to the tail. Scatter the cilantro mixture over the fish.

Divide the beet linguine among four serving plates. Set the weakfish next to the linguine and serve immediately. If desired, garnish with sprigs of fresh rosemary or fennel.

4 SERVINGS

4 medium beets
4 tablespoons rice wine vinegar
1 tablespoon brown sugar
4 scallions, finely sliced
2 tablespoons cracked black pepper
2 tablespoons finely chopped fresh
   cilantro
4 weakfish (about 1 pound each), cleaned,
   scaled, and head removed
4 tablespoons Red Pepper Oil (see Index)
Salt and freshly ground black pepper
Sprigs of fresh rosemary or fennel, for
   garnish (optional)

The red mullet is the superstar of the goatfish family. This extremely nutri-tious white fish is best prepared when very fresh and as simply as possible. I first tasted the savory fish at a roadside café near Malaga, Spain, where I was served a brilliant red mullet that had just been pulled from the sea and cooked on a hot grill. Although I was only a boy at the time, it was a meal I've never forgotten.

4 SERVINGS

4 red mullet (about 1 pound each), with
   skin, cleaned and scaled
2 tablespoons light vegetable oil
1 tablespoon sugar
1 tablespoon finely sliced fresh ginger
4 ripe pears, peeled, cored, and cut
   lengthwise into 8 pieces
1 tablespoon champagne vinegar
1 cup dry white wine
Salt and freshly ground black pepper
Fresh fennel, for garnish (optional)

Preheat the oven to 400 degrees F.

Lay the mullet on a flat surface and, with a sharp knife, make three ½-inch-deep chevron slices on both sides of each fish. Sprinkle with salt and pepper.

Heat the oil in a deep ovenproof skillet over moderately high heat. When the oil is hot, place the mullet in the pan and sear each side for about 1 minute. Remove the fish from the pan and set aside.

To the skillet, add the sugar and ginger, and cook until the sugar dissolves. Arrange the pear slices in the pan so that they fan out from the center. Sprinkle the pear slices with the vinegar, then set the mullet on top of the pears. Add the wine and bring the mixture to a rolling boil. Cover the pan and place in the hot oven for 10 minutes.

Remove the fish from the pan and keep warm. Check the consistency of the pears. If the slices are not tender, poach them in the wine-ginger stock on top of the stove over low heat until soft.

Divide the pear slices among four serving plates and arrange in a fan pattern. Set a mullet beside the pears and drizzle the wine-ginger stock around the edges of the fish. Garnish with fennel, if desired.

The kidney-shaped flageolet bean, which grows in both France and Italy, is sold mainly in specialty stores in this country. Although the flageolet is considered the premier dried bean, any small green or white bean can be substituted. In this recipe the young and tender green legume enhances the mild, pleasant flavor of the hake darnes, or steaks.

4 SERVINGS

1 tablespoon extra-virgin olive oil
1 large onion, finely chopped
4 cloves garlic
1 bay leaf
4 sprigs fresh thyme
1 cup dry flageolet beans
4 large ripe tomatoes, peeled, seeded, and diced
3 to 4 cups Chicken Stock (see Index)
½ teaspoon finely chopped fresh rosemary
1 tablespoon canola oil
4 hake steaks, with skin, about 10 ounces each
Salt and freshly ground black pepper

In a large stainless-steel pot, heat the olive oil over moderately high heat. When the oil begins to release its aroma, add the onion, garlic, bay leaf, and thyme. When the onion is translucent, stir in the flageolets, tomatoes, and 3 cups chicken stock. Bring the mixture to a boil, then reduce the heat and simmer, covered, until the beans are tender, approximately 2 hours. Add additional chicken stock if necessary. When the beans are fully cooked, adjust the seasoning with salt and pepper; discard the garlic. Remove the flageolets from the heat and set aside while preparing the hake.

Preheat the oven to 350 degrees F.

In a small bowl, combine the rosemary with ½ teaspoon freshly ground black pepper and a pinch of salt. Sprinkle both sides of the hake with the seasoning mixture.

Heat the canola oil in a large, heavy, ovenproof skillet. When almost smoking, place the steaks in the pan and quickly sear on both sides. Transfer the skillet to the hot oven and roast for about 10 minutes; the steaks are done when the spine pulls easily away from the flesh.

Remove the steaks from the oven and let sit for 5 minutes before peeling off the skin.

Spoon the flageolets onto the center of a platter and arrange the steaks on top.

The chevron slices in the skin of the herrings in this entrée serve a practical as well as decorative purpose. This fish is so delicate that lengthy cooking would cause the skin to disintegrate. Slashes cut into each side help expedite the cooking process.

Preheat the oven to 400 degrees F.

Rinse the herrings inside and out and pat dry with paper towels. Lay the herrings on a flat surface, and, with a sharp knife, make three ½-inch-deep chevron slices on both sides of each fish. Season with salt and pepper, then rub Red Pepper Oil over the skin.

Place the herrings on a baking sheet or shallow roasting pan and bake in the hot oven until the skin turns crisp, about 5 minutes. Remove from the oven and let rest.

To make the salad dressing, in a blender or food processor, combine the bell pepper, onion, garlic, olive oil, vinegar, a pinch of salt, and a pinch of pepper. Purée on high speed for about 1 minute. Strain through a fine sieve into a large bowl and set aside.

Rinse and drain the lettuce and tear into bite-size pieces. Toss in the dressing.

To serve, place a bed of lettuce on each of four serving plates and arrange two herrings on top.

Note: Dust any roe with all-purpose flour and sauté in a tablespoon of cooking oil until lightly browned. Serve as a garnish for the herrings.

❦

4 SERVINGS

8 herrings (4 to 6 ounces each), cleaned
    and scaled, any roe reserved (see Note)
Red Pepper Oil (recipe follows)
1 red bell pepper, seeded and halved
½ Bermuda onion, roughly chopped
1 clove garlic
1 cup extra-virgin olive oil
⅓ cup malt vinegar
2 bunches red oak-leaf lettuce
2 heads Boston bibb lettuce
Salt and freshly ground black pepper

Combine the olive oil and red pepper in a small saucepan. Warm over low heat for 30 minutes.

Transfer to a blender and blend the pepper into the oil. Pour the flavored oil into a glass container and store indefinitely in the refrigerator.

RED PEPPER OIL

MAKES 2 CUPS

2 cups extra-virgin olive oil
2 tablespoons crushed red pepper

Various fish are passed off as pompano, which accounts for the widely varying reports on its flavor. A true pompano has sweet, somewhat oily, white meat. I tasted pompano for the first time during a visit to Florida and was immediately intrigued.

4 SERVINGS

8 ounces shelled fresh peas
1 tablespoon sugar
1 teaspoon unsalted butter
24 fresh mint leaves, finely shredded
2 tablespoons plain yogurt
¼ cup light vegetable oil
4 skinless pompano fillets, 6 to 8 ounces each
Salt and freshly ground black pepper
Fresh mint and strips of red bell pepper, for garnish (optional)

Place the peas in a small saucepan. Pour in enough water to cover the peas, then add the sugar, a pinch of salt, and the butter. Bring the liquid to a boil, lower the heat, and simmer for 3 to 4 minutes, until the peas are tender. Drain, reserving the cooking liquid.

Reduce the cooking liquid over high heat for 2 to 3 minutes to form a glaze. Combine the reduced liquid with the peas, mint, and yogurt in a blender or food processor. Purée, then keep the mixture warm until ready to use.

Heat the oil in a large, heavy skillet over moderately high heat. Sauté the pompano fillets in the hot oil for about 3 minutes per side. When the fillets are cooked, remove them from the pan and drain on paper towels.

Just before serving, spoon the minted pea purée onto four serving plates and place a pompano fillet in the center. Garnish with mint and strips of red bell pepper, if desired.

In the Orient, tea is considered an aid to the digestion and accompanies every meal. Borrowing from that tradition, grouper is served here with a homemade tea extracted from commonly available herbs. In the boldly flavored beverage the fresh herbs are suspended in the infusion like seaweed in the tide. This versatile recipe can be adapted to black sea bass or cod, and can be presented either warm or cold.

4 SERVINGS

¼ cup light vegetable oil
4 grouper fillets (preferably scamp grouper), with skin, about 8 ounces each
2 cups shredded napa cabbage (bok choy or savoy cabbage may be substituted)
1 cup shiitake mushrooms, stemmed and finely sliced
½ cup finely sliced onion
1 bay leaf
Pinch of caraway seeds
¼ cup dry white wine
Salt and freshly ground black pepper
Fresh flat-leaf parsley, for garnish
Herb Tea (recipe follows)

Preheat the oven to 450 degrees F.

In a large, heavy, ovenproof skillet, heat the oil to just below the smoking point. Season the fillets with salt and pepper. Place the fillets, flesh side down, in the hot oil for a few seconds. Turn and sear the skin side for a minute. Remove the grouper from the pan and set aside.

Add the cabbage, mushrooms, onion, bay leaf, and caraway seeds to the skillet. Cook over moderate heat until these ingredients are tender, about 5 minutes. Drain and discard any liquid, then stir in the wine.

Place the grouper on top of the cabbage mixture. Cover the pan tightly with foil and place in the hot oven for 5 minutes, until the meat flakes when tested with a fork. Remove the grouper from the pan. Drain off any excess liquid from the cabbage mixture, toss, and adjust the seasoning, if necessary, with salt and pepper.

Place a grouper fillet in the center of each serving plate. Spoon some of the cabbage mixture around the fish and garnish with the parsley. Serve with Herb Tea.

In a heatproof pitcher, combine the basil, mint, and dill. Add the honey and pour in 4 cups boiling water. Let steep for 10 minutes. Serve hot or over ice. Sweeten with additional honey, if desired.

HERB TEA

2 ounces (¾ lightly packed cup) fresh
    basil leaves
2 ounces (¾ lightly packed cup) fresh
    mint leaves
2 ounces (¾ lightly packed cup) fresh dill
¼ cup honey

❧ HAKE FILLETS MARINATED IN HERBED OIL ❧

*H*ake has extremely soft flesh that can be infused with the flavor of any fresh herb with a simple herb-and-oil marinade. Here I call for lavender blossoms, a common flavoring in Middle Eastern cookery, but any herb blossoms can be used instead.

In a small saucepan, combine the oil and herbs. Warm the mixture over very low heat for 30 minutes; do not allow the oil to get hot or the herbs will fry.

Place the hake fillets, skin side down, in a shallow pan. Pour the oil over the fillets and refrigerate for 2 hours. Remove the fillets from the oil, drain, and wipe dry with paper towels.

Preheat the oven to 400 degrees F.

Heat a heavy ovenproof skillet until a drop of oil placed in the pan thins and spreads out quickly. Sear the hake in the pan, flesh side down, for about 1 minute, then turn and sear the skin side.

Cover the skillet and transfer it to the hot oven for 4 minutes. Remove the skillet from the oven but leave it covered for several minutes.

Divide the hake among four plates, sprinkle with shredded chervil, and serve with a crisp green salad.

4 SERVINGS

1 cup extra-virgin olive oil
½ teaspoon finely chopped fresh thyme
    leaves
½ teaspoon finely chopped fresh rosemary
    leaves
¼ teaspoon lavender blossoms
1 bay leaf
4 hake fillets, with skin, about 8 ounces
    each
Finely shredded fresh chervil, for garnish

The mild flavor of the warm-water marine fish called amberjack lends itself to the simple method for curing fish favored by the Scandinavians. In this quick version of gravlax, amberjack—rather than salmon—is cured with salt, sugar, and dill. This recipe is extremely versatile and can be made with other fish and vegetables, such as tuna and finely julienned celery, instead of amberjack and daikon.

4 SERVINGS

¼ cup coarse (kosher) salt

¼ cup sugar

1 cup plus 1 tablespoon chopped fresh dill

2 pounds skinned amberjack fillet

1 medium (1 pound) daikon radish

½ small fresh serrano chile, seeded and finely chopped

2 teaspoons lemon juice

2 teaspoons Oriental sesame oil

In a small bowl, combine the salt, sugar, and 1 cup dill. Place the amberjack in a shallow dish and coat with the dill mixture. Cover with plastic wrap and stack several plates, or the equivalent of about 5 pounds of weight, on top of the fish. Marinate in the refrigerator for 30 minutes.

Rinse the amberjack under cold running water for about 20 minutes to remove the salt. Pat the fish dry and seal in plastic wrap. Freeze for approximately 60 minutes, until the fillet is firm but not frozen solid.

Peel the daikon and shred or grate it as thinly as possibly. Place the daikon in a bowl with the remaining dill and the serrano. Add the lemon juice and sesame oil. Toss the mixture, then shape into four loosely formed cones. Place one cone in the center of each serving plate.

Remove the amberjack from the freezer. Using a mechanical slicer or very sharp knife, shave across the grain of the fish into thin ribbons.

Arrange the shaved amberjack around the daikon. Serve immediately.

This recipe calls for flounder, but any firm-fleshed flatfish, such as plaice, sole, or turbot, can be used. The idea for the mustard seeds harks back to my childhood, when we sprouted mustard and cress seeds in science class to demonstrate germination.

4 SERVINGS

4 tablespoons white mustard seeds
4 flounder (about 1 pound each), cleaned,
    heads removed, and fins trimmed
1 tablespoon extra-virgin olive oil, plus
    more for brushing
4 shallots, finely chopped
1 clove garlic, finely chopped
1 small head bok choy, finely sliced
2 oil-packed sun-dried tomatoes,
    finely julienned
¼ cup dry white wine
Salt and freshly ground black pepper
Mustard Vinaigrette (recipe follows)

Sprout the mustard seeds for 2 days before preparation of the flounder: Dampen a clean cloth and spread it on an oblong tray or baking sheet. Sprinkle the mustard seeds evenly over the cloth. Cover with another damp cloth and place in a dark place for 48 hours, sprinkling the cloth with water periodically to ensure that it remains damp during seed germination. The seeds are ready for use when their tops turn light green. Hold at room temperature until ready to serve; do not refrigerate.

Bone each fish so that all four fillets remain connected at the tail: Place the flounder on a flat work surface and locate the lateral line, the natural line running from the head along the side of the body to the tail. With a sharp knife, make an incision 2 inches from the tail and cut along the lateral line to the head end of the fish. With the knife almost flat, slice the flesh away from the rib bones and cut away the top fillet, leaving it connected at the tail. Rotate the fish 90 degrees and cut away the bottom fillet; do not sever the fillet from the tail. Following the same procedure, remove the fillets on the other side of the fish. Discard the carcass.

Lightly brush two large baking sheets with olive oil. Place two boned flounder on each baking sheet so that each fish resembles a scissor. Position the bottom fillets side by side like two blades and curl the top fillets back like the handle. In this position, the tail will remain upright. Season the fish with salt and pepper.

Preheat the oven to 375 degrees F.

In a heavy skillet, heat 1 tablespoon olive oil over moderately high heat until almost smoking. Sauté the shallots and garlic in the hot oil for about 1 minute, then add the bok choy and sun-dried tomatoes. Cover the pan and cook for 10 minutes over medium heat. Add the wine and reduce for 3 minutes, then remove the mixture from the heat and let cool.

Tuck spoonfuls of the vegetable mixture into the crooks of the curled fillets. Brush the flounder with oil and transfer to the hot oven for 10 to 12 minutes, until the meat is white and firm to the touch.

Remove the fish from the oven and let rest a few minutes before transferring to serving plates. Sprinkle generously with the sprouting mustard seeds and nap with the Mustard Vinaigrette.

❦

Place the mustard in a medium bowl. Whisk in enough oil to form a smooth paste, then gradually add the rest of the oil and the vinegar. Stir in the sugar and parsley. Adjust the seasoning with salt and pepper. Cover and store at room temperature until ready to use.

MUSTARD VINAIGRETTE

1 teaspoon dry mustard
½ cup light canola oil
¼ cup champagne vinegar
½ teaspoon sugar
1 teaspoon chopped fresh parsley
Salt and freshly ground black pepper

Use white asparagus in this recipe if you can find them. Green asparagus will work also, but white ones are milder and less acidic. Cooking the asparagus in milk helps to get rid of any bitterness.

Preheat the oven to 400 degrees F.

Trim the stems of the asparagus so the spears are 5 inches in length. With a vegetable peeler or small knife, scrape the stalks from below the tip to the base to remove the woody skin.

In a large saucepan, combine the milk and 4 cups of lightly salted water; bring the liquid to a rolling boil. Immerse the asparagus in the milk and water, cover, and boil for 2 minutes. Carefully lift the spears out of the pan and plunge into ice water. Drain the asparagus and let dry on paper towels.

Season the flounder on both sides with salt and pepper. Overlap 2 flounder fillets around a bundle of 6 asparagus spears so that just the asparagus tips are exposed. Place on a baking sheet with the ends of the fillets facing down. Repeat with the remaining flounder fillets and asparagus spears. Brush the fish and asparagus with olive oil and roast in the oven for 10 to 15 minutes, until the fish is firm. Remove from the heat and let rest for 5 minutes. Serve with Shrimp Salsa.

❧

Combine all the ingredients in a medium bowl. Serve at room temperature.

The salsa can be made in advance, covered, and refrigerated; return to room temperature before serving.

4 SERVINGS

24 fresh asparagus spears
2 cups milk
8 skinless flounder fillets, about
   3 ounces each
Extra-virgin olive oil, for brushing
Salt and freshly ground black pepper
Shrimp Salsa (recipe follows)

SHRIMP SALSA

8 ounces cooked baby shrimp,
   finely chopped
⅓ cup finely chopped Bermuda onion
1 small jalapeño pepper, seeded and
   chopped
1 large ripe tomato, peeled, seeded,
   and finely diced
1 clove garlic, crushed
1 tablespoon extra-virgin olive oil
1 tablespoon malt vinegar
1 tablespoon finely chopped lemon pulp
1 tablespoon finely chopped mint leaves

Mackerel is a robustly flavored fish that is complemented in this recipe by the mild flavor of the rice and the accompanying Oriental-style dipping sauce. The idea for this recipe came to me while I was eating sushi at a Japanese restaurant in New Orleans. I was watching the chef make box sushi, which is probably the oldest method of making sushi, by quickly and dexterously layering fish and rice inside a wooden box. The layers were pressed together, then the sushi was unmolded, sliced, and served. The rice "cake" in this version can be served as either an appetizer or a light entrée.

4 SERVINGS

1 teaspoon wasabi powder (a Japanese horseradish available in Asian markets)
½ cup soy sauce
1 ounce Japanese pickled ginger (available at Asian markets)
3 cups short-grain rice
3 tablespoons sugar
2 teaspoons salt
5 tablespoons rice wine vinegar
2 tablespoons light vegetable oil
4 mackerel fillets, 4 to 6 ounces each
Salt and freshly ground black pepper

In a small bowl, combine the wasabi, soy sauce, and ginger. Let stand at room temperature while you are preparing the remainder of the dish.

Rinse the rice under cold running water for 15 minutes, then drain. Place the rice and 4 cups water in a large heavy saucepan. Bring the rice to a boil and cook over high heat for 2 minutes. Reduce the heat to medium and cook for 4 minutes. Adjust the heat to low, cover the pan, and simmer for 15 minutes. Remove from the heat and let stand, covered, for 15 minutes.

Place the sugar, 2 teaspoons salt, and vinegar in a small saucepan. Cook over low heat until the sugar and salt dissolve. Remove from the heat and cool to room temperature.

Place the rice in a large bowl. Sprinkle with the vinegar mixture and toss with a wooden spoon until the rice begins to cool and becomes shiny. Cover the bowl with a damp cloth and keep warm.

Line two 8-inch dinner plates with plastic wrap and set aside.

In a heavy frying pan, heat the oil to nearly smoking. Sprinkle the mackerel with salt and pepper on both sides and place in the hot oil. Fry the fillets over high heat until the skin turns crispy, about 2 minutes. Remove from the pan and drain on paper towels. Keep the fish warm, but do not cover or the skin will lose its crispiness.

Spread a layer of rice about ½ inch thick on each prepared dinner plate and press into place. Arrange the mackerel fillets in a single layer across the center of the rice on one plate. Quickly invert the second plate onto the first and press firmly. Remove the top plate and plastic wrap.

Invert the rice and mackerel cake onto a wooden cutting board. Remove the base plate and plastic wrap. Cut the cake into wedges and serve with the soy and ginger sauce.

❦ WHITEBAIT WITH OATMEAL ❦

Whitebait does not refer to a single species, but rather to a traditional English dish that is a mixed bag of tiny, completely edible fish. A combination of smelts, anchovies, herrings, and other small or immature fish can be purchased at most seafood markets.

In a small bowl, combine the whitebait and milk. Cover the bowl and refrigerate for 1 hour. Drain the whitebait in a colander.

In a shallow bowl or pie pan, combine the oatmeal, salt, and pepper. Set the mixture aside.

Heat the oil to about 375 degrees F. in a deep frying pan.

Dust the whitebait with the oatmeal mixture and fry for 1 to 2 minutes in the hot oil, until crisp and golden brown. Drain on cloth towels and sprinkle with paprika.

Place the dill sprigs in the hot oil and fry until crisp, about 15 to 30 seconds. Place the whitebait and dill on napkin-lined plates and serve immediately with wedges of lemon or lime.

4 SERVINGS

8 ounces whitebait (see above)
1 cup milk
¼ cup finely ground oatmeal
Dash of salt
½ teaspoon freshly ground black pepper
1 cup canola oil
1 teaspoon paprika
10 fresh dill sprigs
2 lemons or limes, cut into wedges

Since oily fish turn rancid rather quickly, it's important to use your senses when shopping for fresh sardines. First, examine the skin of the fish—it should be uniformly silver and free of any yellow blotches. Next, check that the flesh is firm, not mushy, to the touch. Finally, give the fish a whiff; if the smell is acrid, the fish has started to spoil.

Preheat the oven to 375 degrees F.

Heat 2 tablespoons olive oil in a small skillet over moderately high heat. When the oil is hot, add the garlic and sauté for about 1 minute, until tender. Add the wine, raisins, and sun-dried tomatoes. Cook for another minute, then remove the pan from the heat and add the parsley and pepper. Let the mixture cool to room temperature, then fold in the brioche crumbs.

Using a sharp knife, make an incision on the underbelly of the sardines and open the fish. Stuff each sardine with the brioche mixture and place on a baking sheet. Brush the fish with olive oil and roast in the hot oven for 10 minutes.

Remove the sardines from the oven and serve immediately, or refrigerate and serve cold. Garnish with thyme, if desired.

4 SERVINGS

2 tablespoons extra-virgin olive oil, plus more for brushing
2 cloves garlic, finely chopped
¼ cup dry white wine
¼ cup golden raisins
2 tablespoons finely shredded oil-packed sun-dried tomatoes
1 teaspoon finely chopped fresh parsley
Pinch of freshly ground black pepper
1 cup fine brioche crumbs
16 sardines, heads and tails removed, scaled
Fresh thyme, for garnish (optional)

With its transposed eye and twisted mouth, the plaice is not particularly pretty, but don't let its appearance put you off. This species is one of the most commercially important flatfishes in the world. When I was growing up my mother served baby plaice either sautéed or grilled. Europeans typically enjoy plaice battered and deep-fried, but I prefer a coating of brunoise, or finely diced vegetables.

4 SERVINGS

8 skinless plaice fillets, about 4 ounces each
¼ cup finely diced yellow squash
¼ cup finely diced zucchini
¼ cup finely diced carrot
1 teaspoon egg white
1 tablespoon extra-virgin olive oil
2 shallots, finely chopped
1 cup dry white wine
2 cups Fish Stock (see Index)
4 tablespoons heavy cream
2 teaspoons finely chopped fresh parsley
Salt and freshly ground black pepper

Preheat the oven to 375 degrees F.

Sprinkle the fillets on both sides with salt and pepper. In a small bowl, toss the squash, zucchini, and carrot with the egg white. Press the vegetable mixture onto both sides of the fillets.

Heat the oil in a large ovenproof sauté pan over moderately high heat. When the oil is hot, add the shallots and cook until transparent, about 5 minutes. Lay the fillets on the sautéed shallots, then pour the wine and stock around the fish. Sprinkle with salt and pepper. When the liquid reaches a boil, cover the pan and transfer it to the hot oven for 5 to 7 minutes.

Carefully remove the fillets from the pan and drain on paper towels; the plaice is very delicate and should be handled gently. Place the pan over high heat and reduce the liquid by slightly more than half. Stir in the cream and parsley, and adjust the seasoning with salt and pepper.

To serve, coat four dinner plates with sauce and carefully place 2 fillets in the center of each plate.

Cod, until recently perceived as a poor man's fish, has never received proper credit for its robustly flavored, flaky white flesh. This North Atlantic species is used far more in Europe than in North America. In fact, in England it is the basis for the ever-popular fish and chips. Here cod stars in a hearty, cold weather dish accompanied by a sauce that begs to be mopped up with a chunk of fresh bread.

4 SERVINGS

4 tablespoons extra-virgin olive oil
4 cod steaks, with skin, about 8 ounces
  each
2 medium leeks, white part only, finely
  sliced
1 cup Fish Stock (see Index)
½ cup dry white wine
1 bay leaf
1 sprig fresh thyme
¼ cup heavy cream
Salt and freshly ground white pepper
½ cup blanched rondelles (rings) of leek,
  for garnish
Cracked black pepper, for garnish

Preheat the oven to 375 degrees F.

In a large, heavy, ovenproof skillet, heat the oil to just below the smoking point. Season the cod steaks on both sides with salt and white pepper. Sear the steaks for about 2 minutes per side in the hot oil. Remove from the pan and set aside.

Add the leeks to the hot skillet and sauté until soft. Stir in the stock, wine, bay leaf, and thyme. Arrange the cod steaks on top of the leek mixture, cover the pan, and place in the hot oven. Bake for 10 minutes, then remove the steaks from the pan and keep warm.

Return the skillet to the stovetop and add the cream. Over medium heat, reduce the cream by half. Adjust the seasoning with salt and white pepper to taste.

Cod steaks may be served with the bone in, but for easier eating, remove the bone before serving. First peel off the skin by curling it around the tongs of a fork, then pierce the central bone with a fork or knife and twist and lift out the bone.

Spoon a bed of the thickened leek mixture onto four individual serving plates and place the cod steaks on top. Garnish with the blanched leek and cracked black pepper.

This is an adaptation of "Whiting in Anger," a classic dish in which a whole whiting is deep-fried so that it appears to be biting its own tail. I've revised the original recipe so that the fish is baked rather than fried, which means that I can serve the whiting with a luxurious creamed cucumber sauce without worrying about excessive fat.

Preheat the oven to 375 degrees F. Thread a toothpick through the tail of each fish near the fin, then pass it through the bottom jaw, so it appears as though the whiting is biting its own tail. Set the fish upright on a baking sheet and rub with the sesame oil.

Bake in the hot oven for 5 minutes, then gently peel off the skin between the gill and the tail. Sprinkle the whiting with the sesame seeds and return to the oven for 5 additional minutes or until flaky and opaque. Remove from the heat and let cool.

When cool, carefully remove the toothpicks and serve on a bed of Creamed Cucumbers.

4 SERVINGS

4 whiting (about 1 pound each), cleaned and scaled, head and tail intact
4 tablespoons Oriental sesame oil
4 tablespoons sesame seeds
Creamed Cucumbers (recipe follows)

♥

Place the cucumber slices in a small bowl and sprinkle with the salt. Let sit for 20 minutes, then rinse thoroughly under cold running water and wrap in a clean cloth to drain.

Melt the butter in a medium sauté pan over moderately high heat. When hot, add the shallots, bay leaf, and garlic. Cook until the shallots are clear and soft. Add the drained cucumbers and sauté over moderately high heat for 5 minutes, until the cucumber becomes glossy. Remove the cucumber mixture from the pan and set aside.

To the hot pan, add the wine and cream. Reduce the amount of liquid by half over medium-high heat, then season with salt and white pepper to taste. Return the cucumber mixture to the pan and toss gently. Serve warm.

CREAMED CUCUMBERS

2 European cucumbers, peeled, halved lengthwise, seeded, and finely sliced
¼ cup salt
2 tablespoons unsalted butter
4 shallots, finely chopped
1 bay leaf
2 cloves garlic, crushed
½ cup dry white wine
¼ cup heavy cream
Salt and freshly ground white pepper

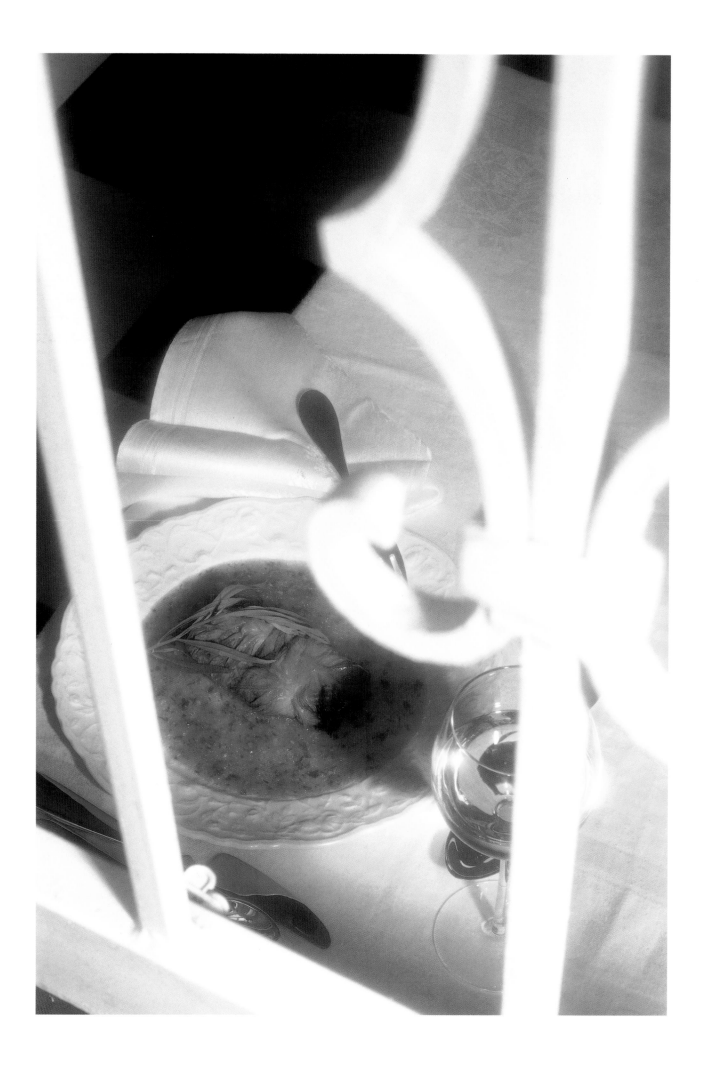

Brill is a popular European flatfish that is sometimes confused with turbot. While closely related, this member of the flounder family is smaller, usually ranging from 2 to 4 pounds. Wrapping the fish in lettuce leaves seals in the moisture and flavor of the fish.

Pour the fish stock into a steamer or Dutch oven fitted with a rack. Bring the stock to a rolling boil, then reduce the heat and simmer.

Season the brill on both sides with salt and pepper and wrap tightly in the lettuce leaves. Place the wrapped fillets in the prepared pan, cover, and steam over the simmering stock for 15 to 20 minutes. When the fish is cooked, remove it from the steamer and keep warm.

To make the vinaigrette, combine the tomatoes, garlic, tarragon, olive oil, lemon juice, and onion in a blender or food processor. Blend on high speed for 2 minutes until puréed. Strain through a fine sieve into a bowl.

To serve, unwrap the brill and discard the lettuce leaves. Place the fillets on serving plates and nap with a light coating of the vinaigrette. Garnish with tarragon sprigs, if desired.

4 SERVINGS

1 quart Fish Stock (see Index)
4 brill fillets, with skin, about 6 ounces
  each
8 to 12 large lettuce leaves
4 large very ripe tomatoes, stemmed
1 clove garlic
2 tablespoons fresh tarragon leaves
½ cup extra-virgin olive oil
Juice of 1 lemon
½ Bermuda onion, finely diced
Salt and freshly ground black pepper
Fresh tarragon sprigs

Because of its delicate texture, seafood connoisseurs agree that scamp is one of the best species of grouper for eating. Here, the fish is roasted and then presented in a manner meant to suggest the fish swimming in its natural habitat. If scamp grouper is unavailable for this piquant recipe, black sea bass or another species of grouper can be substituted.

4 SERVINGS

4 scamp grouper (1 to 1½ pounds each), cleaned, skinned, and head and tail removed
4 teaspoons light vegetable oil
¼ cup honey
½ cup dry sherry
Dash of soy sauce
¼ cup dry mustard
Watercress and Endive Salad (recipe follows)

Preheat the oven to 375 degrees F.

Rub the grouper with the oil on both sides. Open the stomach cavity of the fish and set them upright, as though swimming, on a rimmed baking sheet. Place the grouper in the hot oven for 5 to 7 minutes, then remove from the oven and gently peel off the skin (if the skin does not peel easily, return the fish to the oven and continue to bake for a couple of minutes). Remove any bones from the dorsal area and set the grouper aside.

In a small bowl, blend the honey, sherry, soy sauce, and mustard into a smooth paste. Brush the mixture on the grouper and return to the oven for 10 minutes, until the flesh is flaky and opaque.

Let rest for a few minutes before serving, then present the grouper sitting upright on dinner plates with Watercress and Endive Salad scattered around the fish in little bunches.

❦

WATERCRESS AND ENDIVE SALAD

2 tablespoons pumpkin seeds
2 bunches watercress, torn into bite-size pieces
4 heads Belgian endive, leaves peeled away from the core
½ cup walnut oil
¼ cup champagne vinegar
2 shallots, finely sliced
1 tablespoon Dijon mustard

Spread the pumpkin seeds on a baking sheet and broil until golden brown, about 3 minutes.

Mix the lettuces together in a large bowl. In a cruet or small bowl, combine the oil, vinegar, shallots, and mustard. Toss the lettuce with the dressing and sprinkle with the pumpkin seeds.

Kingfish have no air bladders to resonate and, thus, are the silent members of the croaker family. These bottom feeders are known regionally as whiting, hake, and black mullet. Here, caraway and kümmel add a Nordic touch to what is fundamentally a New England boiled dinner featuring kingfish instead of corned beef.

In this recipe and several others, I specify yellow Finnish potatoes, of which I'm quite a fan. The yellow-jacketed potatoes are quite firm, and when cooked have a buttery texture. If this variety of potato is unavailable, substitute red bliss or small new potatoes.

In a Dutch oven, combine the stock, shallots, bay leaf, peppercorns, and caraway seeds. Bring the stock to a boil, then add the potatoes and kümmel. Simmer the mixture over moderate heat for 10 minutes. Add the leeks, carrots, and fennel, and return the stock to a boil.

Season the kingfish with salt and pepper and slide the fillets into the stock. Cover the pan and remove it from the heat. Let the fish steep in the stock for 5 minutes, then remove the fillets carefully with a slotted spoon and drain on paper towels.

Drain the potatoes, carrots, leeks, and fennel, reserving ¼ cup of the stock. Place 2 kingfish fillets on each serving plate. Garnish with the vegetables and drizzle with the reserved aromatic stock. Serve with Cilantro Mustard for dipping the fish.

Note: Kümmel is an after-dinner *digestif* made with caraway and cumin.

4 SERVINGS

3 cups Fish Stock (see Index)
3 shallots, finely sliced
1 bay leaf
8 whole black peppercorns
1 teaspoon caraway seeds
16 small yellow Finnish potatoes, peeled
½ cup kümmel liqueur (see Note)
2 leeks, white part only, sliced crosswise
    into 1-inch rounds
8 baby carrots
1 cup finely julienned fennel bulb
8 kingfish fillets, with skin, about
    6 ounces each
Salt and freshly ground black pepper
Cilantro Mustard (recipe follows)

❦

In a small saucepan, bring the wine to a boil. Stir in the cilantro and remove from the heat. Transfer the mixture to a small bowl and chill in the refrigerator. When cold, combine with the mustard and serve immediately as a dip or refrigerate until ready to use.

CILANTRO MUSTARD

2 tablespoons dry white wine
1 small bunch cilantro, washed, stemmed,
    and finely chopped
¾ cup champagne mustard

Red drum has achieved worldwide popularity as Cajun blackened redfish. Here the Louisiana fish, also known as channel bass, appears in a version of one of my favorite classical dishes, saumon Chambertin, salmon poached in veal stock and a red wine from Burgundy. Any moderately priced full-bodied red wine can be used instead of Chambertin.

2 tablespoons extra-virgin olive oil
4 red drum fillets, with skin, about
   8 ounces each
2 large onions, finely sliced
1 bay leaf
½ teaspoon fresh tarragon leaves
½ teaspoon fresh thyme leaves
1 clove garlic, crushed
1 cup Chicken Stock (see Index)
1 cup Chambertin Burgundy
Salt and freshly ground black pepper

Preheat the oven to 375 degrees F.

Heat the oil in a large ovenproof frying pan until very hot. Place the drum in the pan, flesh side down, and cook over high heat for about 1 minute. Turn the fillets and cook the skin side for about 1 minute. Cover the pan, transfer to the hot oven, and bake for 10 minutes or until the flesh loses its translucency. Remove the fish from the pan and keep warm until serving.

Place the frying pan back on the stove and add the onions, bay leaf, tarragon, thyme, and garlic. Cook over low heat until the onions turn clear and glossy. Stir in the chicken stock and Burgundy. Bring to a boil, then reduce the heat and simmer the sauce for about 20 minutes, until thickened. Season with salt and pepper to taste.

Spoon the sauce on the base of four dinner plates and set the drum, skin side up, in the center.

Also known as porgy, the sea bream is traditionally cooked in the oven with an assortment of vegetables. In this recipe, the fish is first grilled to add color and flavor and then encased in rice paper and placed in the oven to complete the cooking.

4 SERVINGS

8 skinless sea bream fillets, 4 to 6 ounces each
2 tablespoons extra-virgin olive oil, plus more for brushing
4 (8-inch) round rice paper wrappers (available at Asian markets)
12 ounces (1 ½ cups) beer
1 carrot, finely sliced
1 small Idaho potato, peeled, halved lengthwise, and very finely sliced
3 ribs celery, finely sliced
1 leek, white part only, finely sliced
1 bay leaf
1 clove garlic, chopped
Pinch of fresh savory
½ cup dry sherry
½ teaspoon Body Conscious Pepper (see Index)

Preheat a grill until the coals are very hot.

Brush the sea bream fillets with oil and place on the hot grill just until scored with grill marks, 30 seconds to 1 minute, depending on the heat of the grill. Turn and score the other side. Remove from the heat and transfer to the refrigerator. Chill until set, about 20 minutes.

Place 1 rice paper wrapper on a large plate or tray and pour ¼ cup beer over the wrapper. Top with another wrapper and pour on another ¼ cup beer. Repeat the procedure with the remaining 2 wrappers. Set aside.

Preheat the oven to 400 degrees F.

Heat the remaining 2 tablespoons oil in a heavy skillet. Add the carrot, potato, celery, leek, bay leaf, garlic, and savory, and sauté in the hot oil until the vegetables are tender, about 5 minutes. Add ¼ cup sherry and reduce for 2 to 3 minutes. Remove from the heat and set aside to cool. Remove the bay leaf.

Sprinkle the sea bream fillets with the Body Conscious Pepper. Place a fillet, skin side up, on each rice paper wrapper (see Note at the end of the recipe). Spoon the vegetables down the middle of the fillet and cover with a second fillet, positioned skin side down. Gently pull the rice paper up and over the fish, tucking in both ends securely; the moist rice paper will adhere to itself. With a spatula, transfer one sea bream galette to each of four ovenproof serving plates.

In a small bowl, combine the remaining ½ cup beer and ¼ cup sherry. Sprinkle the galettes with the beer mixture and form a tent over each plate with aluminum foil; seal the edges tightly but do not allow the foil to touch the galettes.

Place the plates in the hot oven for 5 minutes. Remove from the heat and let rest for 5 minutes, then remove the foil and serve immediately.

Note: Rice paper wrappers will invariably tear when you are working with them. Fortunately, they are sticky and can be easily pieced back together.

❦ SKATE WINGS WITH A JULIENNE OF VEGETABLES, ORANGE JUICE, AND SAFFRON ❦

Skate is used in a broad sense to describe any edible species of ray. Only the white gelatinous meat on the pectoral fins, or wings, is consumed. Skate flesh is called "fish lips" by the Chinese, who consider it a delicacy.

In a large pot, combine ½ cup of the vinegar and 1 gallon cold water. Submerge the skate wings in the liquid and soak at room temperature for 2 to 3 hours. Drain the skate and scrape or rub any mucus from the wings. Set the wings aside while preparing the court-bouillon.

Slice 2 of the carrots into coins and place in a stockpot with the onion, leek, peppercorns, salt, bay leaf, remaining vinegar, and 1 gallon cold water. Bring the mixture to a rolling boil, reduce the heat to medium, and cook, stirring, for 5 minutes.

Place the skate in the court-bouillon and poach until the fish is tender and pulls away easily from the cartilage, about 6 to 10 minutes (cooking time will depend on the size of the skate wings). Drain the wings on a cloth and gently strip the skin off both sides with a knife. Keep the wings warm until serving.

Cut the remaining carrot into a fine julienne, then heat the oil over moderately high heat in a heavy skillet. When hot, add the saffron and shallots, and sauté for about 1 minute, until the saffron turns the oil yellow. Stir in the julienned carrot and fennel. Cook for approximately 3 minutes, then add the squash and zucchini. Cook for 2 minutes more, pour in the orange juice, and poach over very low heat for 4 to 5 minutes.

Set one skate wing on each plate and serve the julienned vegetables on the side.

4 SERVINGS

1 cup white wine vinegar
4 skate wings (preferably from 2 common or flapper skate)
3 carrots
1 onion, sliced into rings
1 leek, white part only, sliced into rings
1 teaspoon white peppercorns
1 tablespoon salt
1 bay leaf
1 tablespoon extra-virgin olive oil
Pinch of saffron threads
3 shallots, finely sliced
½ fennel bulb, julienned
½ medium yellow squash, julienned
½ medium zucchini, julienned
½ cup orange juice

The curly "tentacles" of the sole in this whimsical presentation are an allusion to Medusa, one of the mythical snake-haired Gorgons who turned to stone all who looked upon her.

Skin the sole and remove the heads. Using the point of a sharp knife, cut through the flesh along the side fins. Working at an angle, with the knife almost flat, cut the flesh away from the ribs. Turn the fish over and repeat the process so that you end up with two whole fillets attached at the tail. Two inches up from the tail, cut both fillets into eight strips.

Heat the oil in a large, heavy skillet over moderately high heat to just below the smoking point. Dust each fillet with the seasoned flour. Holding the sole by the tail, carefully lower the fish into the hot oil; the strips should curl gently. Cook for 1 minute, then remove the fish from the pan and drain on paper towels. Repeat with the remaining fish.

Place the fennel sprigs in the hot pan and cook briefly, just until crisp. Remove from the pan and drain on paper towels.

Drain any excess oil from the pan and add the butter. When the butter melts, add the capers and when the capers begin to sizzle, add the lemon juice. Cook another minute to warm through.

Arrange the fillets on four plates, presenting each one with the tail positioned at 12 o'clock. Sprinkle the capers around the sole and, if desired, garnish with fresh fennel.

4 SERVINGS

4 dover sole (about 1 pound each), cleaned
  and scaled
½ cup light vegetable oil
All-purpose flour seasoned with salt and
  pepper, for dusting
4 sprigs fresh fennel, plus more for
  garnishing if desired
¼ cup (½ stick) unsalted butter
¼ cup capers, rinsed
Juice of 1 lemon
Salt and freshly ground black pepper

When shopping for this fish, ask your seafood purveyor for sheepshead porgy, a relative of the sea bream that is distinguished by its black stripes. Its unassuming flavor and texture make it perfect for the hearty provincial treatment it gets here.

4 SERVINGS

4 sheepshead (14 to 16 ounces each), cleaned, scaled, and head removed
1 fennel bulb, finely sliced crosswise
2 tablespoons extra-virgin olive oil
2 cups Fish Stock (see Index)
Salt and freshly ground black pepper
White Bean and Lentil Salad (recipe follows)

Preheat the oven to 375 degrees F.

Wash the sheepshead under cold running water. Open each fish, season the inside with salt and pepper, and stuff loosely with fennel. Close the fish and score the skin on both sides with 3 diagonal incisions.

Heat the oil in a large, heavy, ovenproof skillet. When the oil is hot, place the fish in the pan and sear for about 1 minute on each side. Drain the excess oil from the pan and add the fish stock. Cover the pan tightly and transfer to the hot oven for 20 minutes, until the fish flakes when tested with a fork.

Remove the fish from the pan and drain on paper towels. Gently peel away any remaining skin from both sides of the fish.

Mound White Bean and Lentil Salad on four dinner plates. Center a sheepshead on the salad and serve immediately.

❦

WHITE BEAN AND LENTIL SALAD

1 cup dry navy beans
7 or more cups Chicken Stock (see Index)
1¼ cups finely chopped onion
½ teaspoon white pepper
¼ teaspoon crushed red pepper
2 cloves garlic, finely chopped
2 bay leaves
1 cup dry lentils
3 sprigs fresh parsley
1 large onion, very finely diced

Pick through the beans and discard any that are broken or discolored. Place the navy beans in a large saucepan and cover with 6 cups water. Remove any beans that float to the surface. Soak the remainder overnight.

Drain the beans, then return them to the saucepan. Add 4 cups chicken stock, 1 cup finely chopped onion, the white pepper and crushed red pepper, 1 clove finely chopped garlic, 1 bay leaf, and a pinch of salt. Bring the beans to a slow boil and simmer just until tender, 1 to 1½ hours. Drain the beans and cool to room temperature. Discard the bay leaf.

(continued on next page)

Rinse and sort the lentils. In a large saucepan, combine the lentils, the remaining 3 cups chicken stock, ¼ cup finely chopped onion, the remaining clove finely chopped garlic, the remaining bay leaf, and the parsley sprigs. Bring the mixture to a boil, then reduce the heat and simmer, covered, for 45 to 60 minutes. Stir occasionally and add more stock, if necessary. When the lentils are tender, remove the saucepan from the heat. Drain any excess stock, discard the bay leaf, and cool the lentils to room temperature.

In a large bowl, combine the white beans, lentils, finely diced onion, garlic purée, tomatoes, capers, and oregano. Fold in the vinegar, oil, cracked black pepper, and cayenne. Adjust the seasoning with salt to taste and serve at room temperature.

If made in advance, cover and refrigerate; let the salad sit at room temperature for 1 hour before serving.

1 teaspoon Roasted Garlic Purée
   (see Index)
2 medium tomatoes, peeled, seeded, and
   finely diced
1 tablespoon capers, drained
1 teaspoon chopped fresh oregano leaves
2 tablespoons cider vinegar
2 tablespoons extra-virgin olive oil
½ teaspoon cracked black pepper
Pinch of cayenne pepper
Salt

❦ LEMON SOLE
WITH CURRIED POTATOES AND LIME SAUCE ❦

Thanks to the far-flung reaches of the British Empire, Indian food is practically a staple in my homeland. I grew up eating curries in the northwest of England and still appreciate the diversity of the cuisine. The curry powder in the potato recipe can be adapted to personal taste by blending in more or less of the ginger and chile pepper.

Preheat the oven to 375 degrees F. In a large ovenproof sauté pan, heat the butter until melted. Add the shallots and cook over medium heat until translucent, 2 to 3 minutes. Stir in the parsley and wine.

Fold the sole fillets in half lengthwise and place in the pan on top of the shallot mixture. Sprinkle with salt and pepper and cook over moderate heat just until the mixture begins to sizzle, about 30 seconds. Cover with buttered parchment paper and roast in the hot oven for 10 minutes.

To serve, pour the Lime Sauce over the Curried Potatoes and toss gently. Place 2 sole fillets on each plate with the Curried Potatoes on the side.

4 SERVINGS

1 tablespoon unsalted butter
4 shallots, finely sliced
1 tablespoon chopped fresh flat-leaf parsley
¼ cup white wine
8 skinless sole fillets, about 2 to 3 ounces
   each
Salt and freshly ground black pepper
Lime Sauce (recipe follows)
Curried New Potatoes (recipe follows)

(continued on next page)

LIME SAUCE

1 tablespoon sugar

½ cup plus 2 tablespoons dry white wine

Juice of 3 limes, strained

½ cup Fish Stock (see Index)

1 small dried hot red chile, any variety,
    seeded and chopped

2 teaspoons arrowroot

Dash of soy sauce

Zest of 2 limes, grated

In a medium saucepan, cook the sugar over moderately high heat until it begins to brown. Add ½ cup of the wine, the lime juice, fish stock, and chile; the sugar will harden when these ingredients are added. Cook for 2 minutes, stirring, until the sugar dissolves. Combine the arrowroot with the remaining 2 tablespoons wine and stir into the sauce. Simmer, stirring, until thick enough to coat the back of a spoon. Just before serving, add the soy sauce and lime zest. Keep warm.

CURRIED NEW POTATOES

1 teaspoon coriander seeds

¼ teaspoon ground cumin

1 bay leaf

½ small dried hot red chile, any variety,
    seeded

1 teaspoon ground ginger

1 teaspoon cardamom seeds

½ teaspoon mustard seeds

1-inch piece cinnamon stick

1 whole clove

¼ teaspoon ground fenugreek

¼ teaspoon paprika

¼ teaspoon dried lemon peel

¼ teaspoon ground turmeric

1 tablespoon canola oil

1 large onion, finely chopped

4 cups Chicken Stock (see Index)

2 pounds new potatoes, peeled

Prepare a curry powder by placing all the seasonings through the turmeric in a blender or spice grinder and grinding the mixture to a powder. Store the curry powder in a tightly sealed jar.

Heat the canola oil in a large, deep skillet. Add the onion and sauté for several minutes until clear and tender. Stir in 2 teaspoons of the curry powder. Cook for another minute, then add the chicken stock.

Bring the liquid to a boil, add the potatoes, and cook over moderate heat for 20 to 30 minutes, until the potatoes are tender. Remove the pan from the heat and let the potatoes cool in the stock. Drain and serve the potatoes warm or at room temperature.

This august member of the herring family is widely appreciated for its hard roe, a sizable membrane filled with tiny eggs. Here the shad roe is sautéed, but it can also be parboiled, baked, or broiled. Whatever method is used, take care not to overcook the roe or it will become dry and tasteless.

Marinate the shad fillets in 2 tablespoons of the olive oil and 2 tablespoons of the lemon juice for 1 hour in the refrigerator. Marinate the shad roe in the milk for 1 hour in the refrigerator.

Remove the fillets from the marinade and drain on paper towels. Rinse the roe under cold running water, drain, and pat dry.

Heat the remaining tablespoon of olive oil in a heavy skillet over moderately high heat. Dust the roe with flour, add to the skillet, and cook for approximately 2 minutes per side. Remove from the pan and set aside.

In the same skillet, sauté the capers for about 30 seconds. Dice the roe and toss with the capers. Add the remaining tablespoon of lemon juice and the pink peppercorns. Cook, stirring, for 1 to 2 minutes, until the mixture is heated through. Reduce the heat to low and keep the mixture warm until serving.

Preheat a covered outdoor grill. When the coals are hot, add a large handful of the soaked apple wood chips.

Place the shad fillets in the center of the hot grill and close the barbecue. Cook for 3 minutes, then turn and cook the other side, covered, for 2 minutes, until the fish flakes when tested with a fork.

Remove the shad fillets from the grill and divide among four serving plates. Spoon the roe mixture onto each fillet and serve immediately.

4 SERVINGS

4 skinned shad fillets, about 8 ounces each
3 tablespoons extra-virgin olive oil
3 tablespoons lemon juice
8 ounces shad roe
2 cups milk
All-purpose flour seasoned with black
    pepper, for dusting
¼ cup capers, drained
1 teaspoon crushed pink peppercorns
Apple wood chips, soaked in water for
    20 minutes (any flavored wood chips,
    such as cherry or mesquite, may
    be substituted)

2

Shellfish

Eating food according to nature's order enhances my enjoyment of it, so despite the advances in modern aquaculture and the subsequent availability of oysters year-round, I am inclined to respect their natural seasonality and eat them only in the cooler months (traditionally, the months that include the letter "r" in their names). For me, this is when they taste best.

For this recipe (shown on preceding pages), I chose the blue point oyster because it is the most readily available in most parts of the this country. If oysters are native to your area, however, I suggest you substitute a fresh local variety.

4 SERVINGS AS AN APPETIZER

4 large shallots, finely diced
1 teaspoon finely chopped fresh parsley
Juice of 2 limes
Pinch of nutmeg
½ teaspoon cracked black pepper
½ cup extra-virgin olive oil
24 oysters in the shell
Fresh dill and strips of lemon peel,
    for garnish (optional)

In a small bowl, combine all the ingredients except the oysters. Set the sauce aside.

Rinse the oysters and, using an oyster knife, pry open the shells. Cut the muscles and remove the oysters from their shells. Discard the top shells.

Place a teaspoon of sauce in each of the bottom oyster shells and replace the oysters. Serve each person six oysters on the half shell, arranged in a tray of crushed ice. Garnish with dill and strips of lemon peel, if desired.

Texturally speaking, this is a recipe in excess. The beluga eggs pop in your mouth, the tender leeks glide over your tongue, and the plump mussels caress your palate. It is sensational!

Before steaming open the mussels I like to soak them briefly in water to which some flour has been added. This process, known as purging, helps to clean any sand out of the mussels.

Scrape the shells of the mussels with a knife to remove the beards and any barnacles. In a large pot, stir the flour into 1 gallon of cold water. Submerge the mussels in the water and let soak for 5 minutes. Drain and rinse thoroughly.

In a large saucepan, combine the garlic, leeks, wine, thyme, and bay leaf. Bring the mixture to a boil, then add the mussels. Cover the pan and cook over high heat for 5 to 7 minutes, shaking the pan occasionally, until the mussels open. Remove the pan from the heat and, using a slotted spoon, transfer the mussels to a bowl. Set the stock aside to cool.

When the mussels are cool enough to handle, pry off and discard the top shells. Loosen the mussels but leave them on the half shell.

Strain the cooled stock through a fine sieve, reserving the liquid and the leeks. Mound the leeks in the center of four to six serving plates. Divide the mussels among the plates, arranging them around the leeks. Spoon a dab of caviar onto each mussel and drizzle with some of the reserved mussel stock.

4 TO 6 SERVINGS

1 quart (about 20) mussels
1 tablespoon all-purpose flour
2 cloves garlic, crushed
2 leeks, white part only, finely shredded
½ cup dry white wine
1 sprig fresh thyme
1 bay leaf
1 ounce (2 tablespoons) Beluga caviar

The combination of lobster, sweet corn, and truffles is an attack on the senses—from the pungent aroma of the oil to the brilliant color contrast of the lobster and corn. I consider this dish an exercise in self-indulgence.

Shuck the ears of corn and carefully remove all the silks. Save eight large green husks for the garnish.

In a large saucepan, combine the milk, sugar, and 4 cups water. Bring the liquid to a rolling boil, then add the corn. Cover the pan and cook for approximately 5 to 8 minutes, until the kernels are tender.

Remove the corn from the water and let cool. Remove the kernels from the cob by gently scraping down the length of the ears with the back of a spoon. Place the kernels in a medium bowl and set aside.

Remove the meat from the claws and tails of the lobsters; cut the tail meat into ½-inch dice; reserve the claw meat. Place the heads and bodies in a plastic bag and freeze them for future use in stock or other recipes. Add the diced lobster to the corn kernels. Shave or grate the truffle over the mixture and toss with the truffled olive oil. Season with black pepper to taste.

Fill the reserved corn husks with the lobster, corn, and truffle mixture and place two filled husks on each of four plates. Garnish each plate with the meat from two claws and serve.

4 SERVINGS

4 ears sweet corn
2 cups milk
1 tablespoon sugar
4 cooked lobsters, about 1½ pounds each
1 small white truffle
¼ cup truffled olive oil (available at specialty food stores)
Freshly ground black pepper

In classical cookery, "galette" refers to the presentation of any mixture, sweet or savory, as a flat round. In this version, wreaths of wafer-thin, crisp potato slices are layered with a filling of crab meat and puréed garlic. Although I enjoy eating all types of crab meat, blue crab meat is particularly well suited to this recipe and many others because it is firm and doesn't break apart and turn to mush as readily as other varieties.

4 SERVINGS

4 heads garlic, unpeeled
2 tablespoons extra-virgin olive oil, plus
    more for brushing
4 large Idaho potatoes, peeled
1 pound blue crab meat, picked over to
    remove any shell and cartilage
Salt and freshly ground black pepper
Baby Artichokes with Lemon Parmesan
    Dressing (recipe follows)
Fresh basil, for garnish (optional)

Preheat oven to 400 degrees F. Rub the garlic bulbs with olive oil and wrap individually in foil. Seal tightly and place in the oven for 15 minutes. Cool, then unwrap and squeeze the pulp into a medium bowl. Set aside.

Trim each potato so that it is 2 to 2½ inches in diameter. Slice each to the approximate thickness of a dime, keeping the slices from each potato together as you work. Brush two baking sheets with oil and reduce the oven temperature to 375 degrees F. On the baking sheets, arrange the slices from each potato into four circles, 3 to 4 inches in diameter, overlapping the slices like shingles, so that the first slice is "locked" into the last slice. Repeat with all four potatoes, making sixteen potato galettes in all.

Place the baking sheets in the hot oven and cook until the potato galettes turn golden brown, 5 to 10 minutes. Remove from the oven and let cool for 10 minutes.

Add the crab meat to the garlic pulp and season with salt and pepper. Spread a third of the crab meat filling on four galettes, being careful not to spread the mixture over the sides. Set another layer of potato galettes on top of the crab meat, then spread with another third of the crab meat filling. Add another layer of galettes and the final layer of crab meat filling. Top the stack with the remaining potato galettes, browned sides facing up.

Return the filled galettes to the oven and bake for about 5 minutes, until the crab meat is heated through (when the mixture is warm, the aroma of garlic will be released).

Serve the galettes accompanied by Baby Artichokes with Lemon Parmesan Dressing. Garnish with basil, if desired.

In a heavy stainless-steel saucepan, bring 8 cups water to a rolling boil. Add the garlic, chile, bay leaf, lemon, and a pinch each of salt and pepper. Drop in the artichokes and cook over medium heat until tender, 8 to 12 minutes. Remove from the heat and let cool in the cooking liquid while preparing the dressing.

In a small bowl, combine the oil, Parmesan, vinegar, parsley, and shallot. Mix well. Adjust the seasoning with salt and pepper to taste.

When the artichokes are cool enough to handle, drain off the water and gently squeeze each artichoke to remove any excess water. Quarter each artichoke and toss in the dressing. Serve immediately.

BABY ARTICHOKES WITH LEMON PARMESAN DRESSING

4 cloves garlic
1 small chile, fresh or dried, such as cayenne or serrano
1 bay leaf
1 lemon, halved
16 baby artichokes, bottoms trimmed and any brown leaves removed
¼ cup extra-virgin olive oil
2 tablespoons freshly grated Parmesan cheese
2 tablespoons cider vinegar
1 tablespoon chopped fresh parsley
1 shallot, finely chopped
Salt and freshly ground black pepper

Though short in stature—4 to 5 inches at best—the slipper lobster is long on flavor. This warm-water crustacean is most widely used in Australia and Thailand, although it is also native to the United States Gulf Coast. If slipper lobsters are not available, two cups of cooked crawfish, shrimp, or lobster meat can be used instead.

4 SERVINGS

8 ounces morel mushrooms, stemmed
2 tablespoons light vegetable oil
24 slipper lobsters
6 shallots, finely diced
2 cloves garlic, finely chopped
1 bay leaf
½ cup brandy
1 cup Fish Stock (see Index)
1 tablespoon unsalted butter
2 very ripe tomatoes, peeled, seeded, and
    finely diced
Pinch of fresh marjoram
½ cup plus 1 tablespoon Madeira
1 small black truffle, finely diced
1 teaspoon arrowroot
Salt and freshly ground black pepper
Tagliatelle (recipe follows)

Rinse the morels thoroughly to remove any grit. Drain and dry on paper towels. Quarter each mushroom lengthwise and set aside.

In a large skillet, heat the oil over moderately high heat until almost smoking. Place the slipper lobsters in the oil with half the shallots, the garlic, and bay leaf. Sauté over high heat for 3 minutes, stirring constantly. Add the brandy to the skillet, then ignite with a kitchen match. Cover the skillet and remove from the heat. Let sit, covered, for 5 minutes.

Remove the lobsters from the pan. Separate the tails from the bodies and split the flesh of the tail lengthwise down the middle without removing the shell. Cover and set aside. Discard the heads and bodies.

Add the fish stock to the skillet and reduce the amount of liquid by half.

In another large skillet, heat the butter until foamy. Add the morels and remaining shallots. Sauté over low heat until the mushrooms are tender, about 2 minutes.

Remove the morels from the skillet with a slotted spoon and set aside. To the pan, add the tomatoes and marjoram. Simmer until the tomatoes soften, then add ½ cup of the Madeira and the truffle. Continue to simmer for 5 minutes.

Add the reduced lobster stock to the tomato mixture; reduce by half.

Stir the arrowroot into the remaining tablespoon of Madeira. Add this mixture to the combined lobster-tomato sauce. When the sauce is thick enough to coat the back of a spoon, after 5 to 10 minutes, fold in the lobsters and morels. Season with salt and pepper to taste, then simmer for 2 minutes. Remove the bay leaf.

Serve in deep soup bowls with the ragout on one side of the bowl and spinach tagliatelle on the other.

❦

Place 2 quarts (8 cups) water in a large pot. Bring to a boil with the salt and oil. Drop in the noodles and cook at a rolling boil until al dente, about 6 minutes or according to the manufacturer's instructions. Remove from heat and add 2 cups cold water. Drain and serve.

TAGLIATELLE

2 teaspoons salt
2 teaspoons extra-virgin olive oil
½ pound dried green spinach tagliatelle

Slipper lobsters

In this health-conscious recipe, potato is used both to simulate the texture of fat and as an emulsifier in lieu of egg yolk. The substitution is borrowed from vichyssoise, a cold leek soup thickened by potato. I experimented with other salad dressings, including blue cheese and tomato, and found that potato can add the smoothness normally provided by egg yolks to any creamy dressing.

Spread the sesame seeds on a shallow pan or rimmed baking sheet. Place directly under the broiler for 1 to 2 minutes, until lightly browned, or toast in a dry skillet over medium heat for 3 minutes. Shake the pan or skillet frequently so that the seeds brown on both sides and do not burn.

Boil the potato in boiling salted water until tender. Drain and use immediately.

Place the anchovy fillets, garlic, lemon juice, olive oil, and hot potato in a blender and purée. Check the consistency of the dressing, which should resemble mayonnaise; add a little water if the mixture seems too thick.

Wash the romaine lettuce and trim any brown leaves. Gently snap each leaf into bite-size pieces and place in a large bowl.

Toss the lettuce with the dressing until well coated. Sprinkle with sesame seeds and Parmesan and Romano cheese. Fold in the crab meat and serve with Fresh Croutons.

❦

4 SERVINGS

2 tablespoons sesame seeds
1 small potato, peeled
4 anchovy fillets, drained
2 cloves garlic, crushed
2 tablespoons lemon juice
½ cup extra-virgin olive oil
2 heads romaine lettuce
1 tablespoon freshly grated Parmesan
  cheese
1 tablespoon freshly grated Romano cheese
1 pound lump crab meat, picked over to
  remove any shell and cartilage
Salt and freshly ground black pepper
Fresh Croutons (recipe follows)

Arrange the bread slices on a baking sheet and toast on one side directly under the broiler. Remove from the heat, then rub with the garlic and brush with the oil on both sides. Return to the broiler and toast the other side. Serve immediately or store in an airtight container for up to a week.

FRESH CROUTONS

8 slices French bread, about ½ inch thick
2 cloves garlic
2 tablespoons extra-virgin olive oil

The lobster featured in this dish is not the North Atlantic variety. Rather, it is a spiny rock lobster that hails from the warm waters of the Mediterranean and Caribbean. Because the flesh of these clawless lobsters degenerates so quickly following capture, live rock lobsters are extremely scarce. Purchase frozen rock lobsters and thaw them slowly over ice, or substitute another clawless lobster species, perhaps one from South Africa or New Zealand.

4 SERVINGS

4 live rock lobsters, about 2 pounds each
1 clove garlic, crushed
Juice of 1 lemon
¼ cup finely diced Bermuda onion
¼ teaspoon freshly ground black pepper
Dash of Tabasco sauce
2 tablespoons extra-virgin olive oil
1 bunch watercress
2 teaspoons sesame seeds
Oriental Vinaigrette (recipe follows)

To kill the lobsters, place a sharp knife on the point of the head between the eyes and push through. Grip the tail with a thick cloth and twist and pull with the other hand to separate the tail from the body. Place the heads and bodies in a plastic bag and freeze them for future use in stock or other recipes.

Make a cut down the center of the meaty side of the tail and set aside. In a shallow dish that is large enough to hold all 4 lobster tails, combine the garlic, lemon juice, onion, pepper, Tabasco, and olive oil. Place the lobster tails in the mixture, flesh side down, and marinate at room temperature for 30 minutes.

Separate the watercress leaves and soak in slightly salted ice water for 5 minutes. Drain on a cloth, then remove and discard the stems. When the watercress is dry, place in a bowl and toss with the sesame seeds. Cover and refrigerate until ready to use.

Light a grill or preheat the broiler.

Remove the lobster tails from the marinade and place them, meat side down, on the grill. Cook for approximately 3 minutes per side, until the shell turns bright red. If using a broiler, place the tails, meat side up, on a baking sheet and broil for 3 minutes.

Remove the lobster tails from the heat and set aside
to let the meat relax for easier shelling. Meanwhile,
toss the watercress and sesame seeds with the
Oriental Vinaigrette.

While the tail meat is still warm, remove it from the
shell and cut into ½-inch dice. Toss the lobster with
the dressed watercress and serve immediately.

Rock lobsters

Combine the ingredients in a small bowl and let sit at
room temperature for 1 hour. Remove the ginger sachet
and squeeze all the juice into the vinaigrette. Stir and use
immediately or cover and refrigerate until ready to use.

ORIENTAL VINAIGRETTE

¼ cup Oriental sesame oil

2 tablespoons rice wine vinegar

2 tablespoons honey

1 tablespoon soy sauce

1 tablespoon finely chopped fresh ginger,
tied in muslin or cheesecloth

As private kitchens become outfitted with restaurant-style equipment, a whole new range of dishes becomes accessible to the home cook. To cut the potatoes in this recipe, you need a commercial vegetable slicer, a chef's tool that operates on the same principle as a woodworker's lathe. The tomatoes that accompany the potato-wrapped shrimp are desiccated, or slowly dried, to bring out their inherent sweetness.

4 SERVINGS

2 large Idaho potatoes, peeled
16 large shrimp, shelled, with heads left on
8 very ripe plum tomatoes
2 cloves garlic, finely chopped
1 teaspoon shredded fresh basil leaves
1 teaspoon cracked black pepper
1 teaspoon finely chopped lime zest
¼ cup extra-virgin olive oil

Using a vegetable slicer, cut the potatoes into thin strands, 12 to 16 inches in length.

Wrap 5 to 6 strands of potato around the tail of each shrimp. Place the wrapped shrimp on a tray, cover with plastic wrap, and freeze overnight.

Preheat the oven to 175 degrees F.

Cut the tomatoes lengthwise and place the slices on a baking sheet.

In a small bowl, blend the garlic, basil, pepper, and lime zest. Sprinkle the mixture on the tomatoes. Cover the tomatoes with parchment paper and place in the oven for at least 12 hours.

Before serving, remove the tomatoes from the oven and increase the temperature to 400 degrees F.

Heat the oil to almost smoking in a heavy ovenproof skillet over moderately high heat. Add the frozen potato-wrapped shrimp to the skillet and quickly brown on both sides. Transfer the skillet to the hot oven for 10 minutes, until the potatoes and shrimp are fully cooked.

Serve each person four potato-wrapped shrimp with warm dried tomatoes on the side.

The porcini is the Rolls-Royce of mushrooms; that is, if you can get good, fresh ones, which can be a problem (see opposite page for tips on evaluating freshness). Also known as boletus edulis, bolete, cep, and cèpe, this pungent woodland mushroom is a flavorful accompaniment to the creamy rice in this entrée.

4 SERVINGS

¾ cup arborio rice (Italian short-grain rice)
24 large white shrimp, peeled and
    deveined (reserve heads and shells)
2 tablespoons extra-virgin olive oil
½ large onion, finely diced
1 clove garlic
1 bay leaf
1 cup dry white wine
2 or more cups Chicken Stock (see Index)
¼ cup freshly grated Parmesan cheese
2 tablespoons freshly grated Romano
    cheese
1 tablespoon shredded fresh basil leaves
Salt and freshly ground black pepper
Sautéed Porcini Mushrooms
    (recipe follows)
Fresh Croutons (see Index)

Place the rice in a fine sieve and rinse under cold running water for 2 minutes. Set aside and drain.

With a sharp knife, split the shrimp down the back, cutting to a depth of about ¼ inch.

Heat the oil in a heavy skillet over moderately high heat. When the oil begins to sizzle, add the shrimp and sauté in the hot oil until pink but not cooked all the way through, about 2 to 3 minutes. Lift the shrimp out of the pan and drain on paper towels. To the skillet, add the onion, garlic, bay leaf, and reserved shrimp heads and shells. Cook over moderately high heat, stirring, for 1 minute; remove and discard the shrimp heads and shells.

Add the rice to the skillet and cook, stirring constantly, until the grains become translucent around the edges and white in the center. Immediately stir in the wine and reduce the heat to medium. When the wine is absorbed, add 1 cup of stock. Cook, stirring constantly, until the stock is absorbed. If the rice is not tender, add another ½ cup of stock and cook until absorbed. Test the rice and, if necessary, add additional stock, while stirring, until the rice is tender yet al dente.

Remove the pan from the heat, then pull out and discard the garlic clove and bay leaf. Fold in the shrimp, Parmesan and Romano cheeses, and basil; season with salt and pepper. Cover the pan and let sit for 2 minutes.

Serve the risotto in shallow bowls with Sautéed Porcini Mushrooms and Fresh Croutons on the side.

❧

Trim and discard the base of the porcini stems, then rinse the porcinis to remove any grit. Drain on paper towels until dry.

Stem the mushrooms and slice the caps ⅛ inch thick. Slice the stems across the diameter into ¼-inch slices.

Heat the oil in a heavy skillet over moderately high heat to almost smoking. Add the shallots and sauté until translucent, stirring constantly. Add the mushrooms and cook for 2 minutes until they begin to soften, then stir in the wine. Season with salt and pepper and cook for another minute.

Garnish the warm porcini with parsley and serve.

SAUTÉED PORCINI MUSHROOMS

To evaluate the freshness of porcini mushrooms, first check that their weight is fairly heavy relative to their size. Then break open one or two caps and look for worms, which will be clearly visible if present.

1 pound fresh porcini mushrooms
1 tablespoon extra-virgin olive oil
2 shallots, finely chopped
2 tablespoons dry white wine
1 tablespoon finely chopped flat-leaf
    parsley
Salt and freshly ground black pepper

The shellfish anomaly featured in this dish is a blue crab harvested during molting. Once the crustacean has shed its protective shell, it is almost entirely edible. Since you couldn't get soft-shell crabs where I grew up in England, I didn't experience them until my arrival in Louisiana in 1980. I became hooked immediately and in the years since have experimented with many soft-shell crab recipes.

4 SERVINGS

4 live jumbo soft-shell crabs
All-purpose flour, for dusting
4 tablespoons light vegetable oil
1 cup Chicken Stock (see Index)
1 medium Idaho potato, peeled and sliced
1 cup dry white wine
2 tablespoons extra-virgin olive oil
4 ribs celery (from the heart), trimmed
    and finely sliced
1 teaspoon pink peppercorns
Salt and freshly ground black pepper

Preheat the oven to 400 degrees F.

Clean the crabs by removing the eyes and gills and trimming the tails. Season lightly with salt and pepper, then dust with flour.

Heat the vegetable oil in a large sauté pan over moderately high heat until almost smoking. Place the crabs, shell side down, in the hot oil and cook for 2 minutes. Turn and cook the other side for 2 minutes, then transfer to the oven for about 5 minutes, until the crabs are firm. Remove from the oven and keep warm while preparing the sauce.

In a medium saucepan, combine the chicken stock, potato, and wine. Bring the mixture to a rolling boil and cook until the potato slices fall apart. Pour this mixture into a blender or food processor and purée until smooth.

Heat the olive oil in a medium skillet over moderately high heat until it begins to sizzle, then add the celery and pink peppercorns. Cook until the celery is glossy, about 5 minutes. Stir in the thickened chicken stock and bring the mixture to a rolling boil. Reduce, if necessary, until thick enough to coat the back of a spoon.

To serve, spoon the sauce onto four dinner plates and place a crab in the center of each.

The following is my conscious effort to strip the superfluous fat out of the frittata. The naturally creamy texture of the crab meat allows for the elimination of egg yolks from this Italian omelet.

4 SERVINGS

2 egg whites
½ teaspoon sugar
1 pound lump crab meat, picked over to remove any shell and cartilage
1 small red bell pepper, seeded and very finely diced
2 scallions, very finely julienned
1 tablespoon canola oil
Salt and white pepper
Artichoke Dressing (recipe follows)

Preheat the oven to 400 degrees F.

In a stainless steel or glass mixing bowl, whip the egg whites to soft peaks, then beat in the sugar. Working quickly, fold in the crab meat, bell pepper, and scallions; season with salt and pepper to taste.

Heat the oil to almost smoking in a large cast-iron skillet over moderately high heat. Pour the crab meat batter into the hot skillet, then immediately transfer the pan to the oven. Bake for 15 minutes, until lightly browned and set.

Serve the crab meat frittata, sliced into wedges, from the skillet. Set small bowls of Artichoke Dressing alongside for dipping.

❣

ARTICHOKE DRESSING

1 pound baby artichokes, stemmed and leaves trimmed
¼ cup Red Pepper Oil (see Index)
1 clove garlic
2 tablespoons champagne vinegar
1 teaspoon Dijon mustard
1 tablespoon dry sherry
1 tablespoon lemon juice
Salt and freshly ground black pepper

Boil the artichokes in lightly salted water for 20 to 35 minutes, until the bottoms are tender and the leaves pull out easily.

Place the artichokes and the remaining ingredients through the lemon juice in a blender or food processor. Add a pinch each of salt and pepper and purée the mixture. Strain through a fine sieve, adjust the seasoning, and refrigerate until ready to use.

Of all the recipes for cooked crawfish, this simple and unadorned Louisiana-style recipe is one of the most delicious. The small crustaceans are boiled in an aromatic stock along with vegetables and citrus fruit. Then the "mud-bugs," as they are known in their native state, are served in their shells on newspaper instead of plates.

Place the onions, celery, garlic, oranges, lemons, salt, black pepper, bay leaves, dill seeds, allspice, cloves, and cayenne pepper in a 10-gallon pot. Add 5 gallons water. Cover and bring to a boil over high heat. Add the potatoes and corn. Cover and cook for about 6 minutes, then stir in the crawfish. Cook, covered, for another 8 minutes. Turn off the heat and let the mixture sit, covered, for 25 minutes.

Before serving, drain and discard the cooking liquid. Cover a table with several thicknesses of newspaper. Spread the crawfish, fruits, and vegetables down the center of the table. Place small bowls of Kumquat Relish on the side as a condiment.

4 SERVINGS

3 large onions, roughly chopped
2 bunches celery, roughly chopped
6 heads garlic, unpeeled
6 oranges, halved
6 lemons, halved
½ cup salt
½ cup freshly ground black pepper
10 bay leaves
½ cup dill seeds
¾ cup ground allspice
½ cup whole cloves
¾ cup cayenne pepper
3 pounds new potatoes in their jackets, scrubbed
6 ears sweet corn, shucked and halved
12 pounds live crawfish, soaked in cold water for 25 minutes and drained
Kumquat Relish (recipe follows)

❦

Wash and dry the kumquats. With a sharp knife, slice the kumquats across the diameter to the approximate thickness of a penny. Strain any kumquat juice and reserve.

In a small saucepan, heat the oil over moderately high heat to almost smoking. Add the kumquat slices and sauté for 5 minutes. Stir in the garam masala and cook for a couple of minutes, until smooth, then add the reserved kumquat juice, honey, and brown sugar. Cook for 5 minutes, stirring continuously. Remove from the heat and add the red wine vinegar. The texture of the relish should resemble a light mayonnaise. Serve either hot or cold as a condiment.

KUMQUAT RELISH

2 pounds kumquats
2 tablespoons canola oil
3 tablespoons garam masala (an Indian spice mixture available at Asian markets)
1 cup honey
½ cup brown sugar
2 tablespoons red wine vinegar

Prior to refrigeration, potting was a practical method of preserving meat. The technique became part of English culinary tradition, and in my jolly old homeland cooked meats are still puréed, packed into molds, and sealed in fat—the British equivalent of pâté. Here, in this much lighter rendition of the time-honored practice, shellfish is substituted for the meat and only a modicum of fat is required.

4 SERVINGS

¼ cup (½ stick) unsalted butter
Juice of 2 lemons
2 tablespoons ketchup
Pinch of ground white pepper
Pinch of ground black pepper
½ teaspoon ground nutmeg
Dash of Tabasco sauce
Dash of Worcestershire sauce
8 ounces cooked baby shrimp
8 ounces lump crab meat, picked over to remove any shell and cartilage
4 cooked artichokes (recipe follows)
Fresh fennel, for garnish (optional)

It is essential that all the ingredients be at room temperature before beginning preparation of the potted shellfish.

In a large mixing bowl, blend together the butter, lemon juice, ketchup, white pepper, black pepper, nutmeg, Tabasco, and Worcestershire sauce. Fold in the shrimp and crab meat. Divide the mixture among four ½-cup ramekins. Cover the molds with plastic wrap and refrigerate overnight.

Set a warm prepared artichoke on each of four plates. Just before serving, run a knife around the edge of each mold, invert, and unmold into the center of the artichoke. Garnish with fennel, if desired. Serve immediately.

❦

COOKED ARTICHOKES

4 medium artichokes
1 small lemon, cut into 4 slices
1 tablespoon all-purpose flour
4 cloves garlic
¼ cup extra-virgin olive oil
1 teaspoon crushed red pepper
Pinch of salt

Slice off the tops of the artichokes and remove any brown leaves. With kitchen shears, trim the sharp points from the rest of the leaves. Use a sharp knife to remove the stalks, so that the artichokes will sit upright. Place a slice of lemon on the base of each artichoke and secure with kitchen string tied across the leafy top.

Fill a large pot with 2 gallons of cold water. Sprinkle in the flour and stir with a whisk until dissolved. Add the garlic, oil, red pepper, and salt. Bring the mixture to a boil, then immerse the artichokes in the liquid. Cook for 20 to 30 minutes, until the base is tender. Remove the artichokes from the pan and let cool for 5 minutes.

Discard the lemon and string, then pull out the tender pale green leaves in the core of the artichokes. Using a spoon, twist and scoop out the furry choke. Serve the artichokes warm.

In this dish, pasta-encased seafood nuggets are dressed with oil and vinegar instead of a heavy sauce. It is an entrée that can be presented either hot or cold and never fails to please my guests, even those who are counting calories.

4 SERVINGS

4 egg yolks

½ cup plus 3 tablespoons extra-virgin olive oil

½ teaspoon plus a pinch of finely chopped fresh basil leaves

1 pound (4 cups) unbleached flour

8 ounces peeled and deveined shrimp

8 ounces sea scallops

¼ cup Tomato Concasse (see Index)

¼ cup freshly grated Parmesan cheese

3 tablespoons champagne vinegar

2 radishes, very finely sliced

1 teaspoon chopped fresh parsley

Salt and freshly ground white pepper

In a small bowl, combine the egg yolks, ¼ cup of the olive oil, ½ cup water, and a pinch of finely chopped basil; lightly whip the mixture.

Sift the flour with a pinch each of salt and white pepper onto a pastry board. Make a well in the center of the flour and pour the yolk mixture into the well. Gradually incorporate enough flour into the yolks to form a soft dough; add additional water as necessary.

Knead the dough for 8 to 10 minutes, until it is smooth and elastic. Form the dough into a ball, cover with plastic wrap, and let rest for 2 hours in the refrigerator.

Heat 1 tablespoon of the olive oil in a medium skillet over moderately high heat until it releases its aroma. Sauté the shrimp and scallops in the hot oil until the shrimp turn pink, 2 to 3 minutes. Remove the shrimp and scallops from the pan and let cool.

Reduce any liquid in the skillet by half, then add the tomato concasse and the remaining ½ teaspoon basil. Cook the concasse over moderately high heat until all the liquid has evaporated, then remove from the heat.

Chop the shrimp and scallops into a fine dice and fold into the concasse. Season with salt and pepper and refrigerate for 30 minutes. Blend the Parmesan into the chilled filling and keep cold until ready to use.

On a lightly floured pastry board, roll half the dough into a thin 15-inch-square sheet. Set the sheet aside and repeat the process with the remaining dough. Let rest an additional 20 minutes.

Dot teaspoons of filling 1½ inches apart, in rows, on one of the sheets of dough. Cover with the other sheet and press firmly between the mounds of filling. Cut between the mounds with a fluted pastry wheel or sharp knife. Place the ravioli on a floured tray.

Bring 1 gallon water and 2 tablespoons of the olive oil to a boil in a large pot. Cook the ravioli in the boiling water until al dente, 5 to 6 minutes.

While the pasta is cooking, combine the remaining ¼ cup olive oil and the champagne vinegar in a large bowl.

Drain the cooked ravioli and toss in the oil and vinegar. Sprinkle with the radish and parsley. Serve immediately or refrigerate and serve cold.

In this dish, grilled scallop kebabs rise from the serving platter for a three-dimensional effect. It's a real attention-grabber.

Light a grill or preheat the broiler.

Pick the leaves off 6 inches of the rosemary, leaving 2 inches of leaves on one end of each sprig. Discard or save the leaves for another use.

Skewer 5 scallops on the leafless part of each sprig and season with Body Conscious Pepper. Grill or broil the scallop kebabs for 2 minutes, turning once.

Place a bed of Basmati Rice on a serving platter. Carefully stand the skewers in the rice, scallops down, rosemary leaves up, so that the kebabs lean against each other and form a pyramid. Serve immediately.

4 SERVINGS

4 (8-inch) fresh rosemary sprigs
20 large sea scallops (about 2 pounds)
Pinch of Body Conscious Pepper (see Index)
Basmati Rice with Turmeric and Almonds (recipe follows)

❦

BASMATI RICE WITH TURMERIC AND ALMONDS

Preheat the broiler. Place the rice in a colander and rinse under cold running water while rubbing the grains together with your fingers. When the water runs clear, turn off the faucet and drain the rice thoroughly.

Spread the almond slices on a rimmed baking sheet and broil for 3 to 5 minutes, until golden brown. Remove from the broiler and let cool.

Heat the vegetable oil to almost smoking in a large, heavy skillet over moderately high heat. Add the onion and bay leaf, and sauté until the onion becomes glossy. Stir in the turmeric, then add the cloves and 2 cups water. When the mixture comes to a rolling boil, stir in the rice. Reduce the heat to low, cover, and cook for 15 minutes.

After 15 minutes, lift the lid and check the rice. If any liquid remains, re-cover and cook an additional 5 minutes. When the rice has absorbed all the liquid, remove the pan from the heat, re-cover, and let steam for several minutes.

Fold the toasted almonds into the rice and adjust the seasoning with salt and pepper. Add the olive oil and fluff with a fork to separate the grains. Serve warm.

1 cup basmati rice
¼ cup almond slices
2 tablespoons light vegetable oil
1 onion, finely chopped
1 bay leaf
½ teaspoon turmeric
2 whole cloves
1 teaspoon extra-virgin olive oil
Salt and freshly ground black pepper

This salad is a signature dish of the Caribbean Islands. It must be served quite soon after preparation, lest the acids in the lime juice react with the protein in the conch, resulting in tough and rubbery meat. I particularly like the flavor of Vidalia onions here, but any other mild, sweet onion, such as Bermuda or Maui, can be used instead. The meat of the large univalve is sold shucked or in the shell, and should smell sweet, not fishy. Since the flesh is tough, it must be tenderized before cooking.

4 SERVINGS

1 pound fresh conch meat
1 Vidalia onion, finely chopped
½ cup lime juice
Zest of 1 lime, finely chopped
4 tablespoons extra-virgin olive oil
1 jalapeño pepper, seeded and finely diced
1 red bell pepper, seeded and finely diced
2 ribs celery, finely diced
Dash of Tabasco sauce
Dash of malt vinegar
1 large ripe tomato, peeled, seeded, and finely diced
½ European cucumber, peeled, seeded, and finely diced
10 fresh mint leaves, finely shredded
Pinch of salt
¼ teaspoon freshly ground black pepper
Grilled Radicchio (recipe follows)

Place the conch between sheets of plastic wrap and pound gently with a mallet for about 2 minutes, until limp. Cut the meat into fine julienne with a sharp knife and place in a large stainless-steel bowl. Add the remaining ingredients, cover, and chill. The salad can be refrigerated for up to 2 hours before serving.

Serve the conch salad with Grilled Radicchio on the side.

♥

GRILLED RADICCHIO

1 large head radicchio
1 teaspoon brown sugar
1 tablespoon balsamic vinegar
1 tablespoon extra-virgin olive oil

Cut the radicchio into quarters; rinse thoroughly and drain. Place the lettuce in a large bowl and add the brown sugar, vinegar, and oil. Toss until the radicchio is evenly coated.

Heat a large heavy skillet until a bead of water added to the pan sizzles and pops. Place the radicchio in the pan and sauté for 3 to 5 minutes, turning frequently, until the lettuce is wilted. Serve warm.

Littleneck clams are very small and very tender. They are at their best when served au naturel, accompanied by this tangy dressing (see photograph on following pages).

Preheat the oven to 400 degrees F.

Brush the garlic with oil and wrap in aluminum foil. Seal tightly and place in the hot oven for 15 minutes. Let cool, then squeeze out the soft pulp.

In a mixing bowl, combine the garlic pulp, tomatoes, scallions, oil, lime juice, Tabasco, Worcestershire, and pepper. Mix thoroughly and let stand at room temperature for 1 hour.

Scrub the clam shells and pat dry. Grasp a clam by the hinged part of the shell. Insert the blade of a knife between the shells, and gently slide the knife along the inside to sever the muscle on both sides and release the clam; do not separate the shells. Remove the clam and place in a bowl. Repeat with the remaining 47 clams.

Divide the clam shells among four plates. On the base of each shell, place a spoonful of dressing. Set the clam back in the shell and top with another spoonful of dressing. Sprinkle with chopped parsley and dill, then serve.

4 SERVINGS

4 cloves garlic
4 very ripe tomatoes, peeled, seeded, and
    finely chopped
4 scallions, finely chopped
½ cup extra-virgin olive oil, plus extra for
    brushing
Juice of 4 limes
¼ teaspoon Tabasco sauce
¼ teaspoon Worcestershire sauce
½ teaspoon freshly ground black pepper
48 littleneck clams
Chopped fresh parsley and dill,
    for garnish

Stuffed grapevine leaves are standard fare in the eastern Mediterranean, but this version packed with shellfish and wild mushrooms definitely takes the dish in a new direction. As is so often the case in the kitchen, the creation of this appetizer was strictly spontaneous. One of the cooks brought some grapevine leaves from his home garden, we had a delivery of fresh chanterelles, and crawfish were plentiful—pure kismet! The earthy flavor of chanterelles is a key taste factor, but any wild mushroom, such as morel or porcini, can be used instead.

Preheat the oven to 375 degrees F.

In a heavy skillet, heat the oil over moderately high heat until almost smoking. Add the shallots, garlic, and thyme, and sauté. When the shallots are clear, add the chanterelles and cook over moderate heat for 3 to 4 minutes. Stir in the Madeira and bring the mixture to a slow boil. Remove the chanterelles with a slotted spoon; transfer to a small bowl.

Over high heat, reduce the Madeira mixture by half; it will take about 5 minutes. Add the crawfish and cook for 1 minute. Season with salt and pepper, then return the chanterelles to the mixture, along with any residual mushroom juice. Remove the filling from the heat and set aside while preparing the leaves.

If using fresh grapevine leaves, remove the stems and blanch the leaves in boiling salted water for 3 to 4 minutes; immediately plunge in ice water and drain on paper towels. Vacuum-packed or bottled leaves should be rinsed to remove the brine.

Spread the leaves on a flat surface and place a tablespoon of filling in the center of each leaf. Fold in the edges and roll the leaves into cylinders.

Place the filled leaves in a baking dish. Drizzle with olive oil and bake in the hot oven until heated through, about 5 to 7 minutes.

Divide the stuffed grapevine leaves and the sliced tomato and crumbled feta among four serving plates. Garnish with fresh chives, if desired.

4 SERVINGS

2 tablespoons extra-virgin olive oil, plus more for drizzling
2 shallots, finely chopped
1 clove garlic, finely chopped
Pinch of fresh thyme
8 ounces fresh chanterelles, washed or wiped clean, stemmed, and sliced
½ cup Madeira
1 pound cooked and peeled crawfish tails, finely chopped
16 grapevine leaves (fresh, vacuum-packed, or bottled)
Salt and freshly ground black pepper
1 small ripe tomato, finely sliced
4 teaspoons feta cheese, rinsed and crumbled
Fresh chives, for garnish (optional)

Until recently I never dreamed of barbecuing octopus; instead I thought of the tentacled marine animal in terms of more conventional European dishes, such as sautéed octopus served with rice or pasta. I got the idea for this down-home treatment at a small bistro in Sydney, Australia. Perhaps it will help to win the tasty cephalopod some new fans.

4 SERVINGS

12 baby octopuses, 2 to 3 ounces each
1 daikon radish, top and roots trimmed, peeled, and finely grated
1 ¼ cups honey
¼ cup soy sauce
¼ medium onion, chopped
½ medium green bell pepper, seeded and finely chopped
½ medium red bell pepper, seeded and finely chopped
1 medium tomato, peeled, seeded, and chopped
4 cloves garlic, finely chopped
¾ cup malt vinegar
1 ½ cups prepared chili sauce
2 tablespoons tomato paste
2 tablespoons chili powder
Green Bean Salad (recipe follows)

With a sharp knife, make a slit at the base of the body of each octopus as though to separate it from the tentacles, but do not cut all the way through. At the incision, turn the body sac partially inside out and pull out the innards. Discard the innards and close the body sac. Cut away the eyes and the hard "beak," the skeletal vestige that is buried in the flesh of the tentacles.

Wash the octopuses thoroughly and place in a large bowl with the daikon. Knead the octopuses gently with the daikon for about 7 minutes, until the radish turns a light gray. Rinse the octopuses under cold running water and discard the daikon.

Combine 1 cup of the honey and the soy sauce in a large saucepan with 8 cups water. Bring the liquid to a rolling boil. Using tongs, pick an octopus up by the body sac so that the tentacles hang down. Dip the tentacles into the boiling water 3 or 4 times until they curl and the octopus takes on the form of a ball. Repeat with all the octopuses, then immerse all the whole octopuses in the water at the same time and cook for 7 minutes. During cooking, the skin will turn pink.

Remove the pan from the heat and let the octopuses cool in the water at room temperature for 4 hours.

Make a barbecue sauce by combining the remaining ingredients through the chili powder (including the remaining ¼ cup honey) in a large bowl. Place the octopuses in the sauce and marinate at room temperature for 1 hour.

Heat a grill to very hot. Place the octopuses on the grill and cook for about 5 minutes, turning once, until firm to the touch.

Serve the warm grilled octopus with Green Bean Salad.

Bring 4 cups water to a boil in a large saucepan. Add a pinch of salt. Add the green beans and blanch for 2 to 3 minutes. Drain and chill in a bowl of ice water. Drain and spread on paper towels to dry.

When the beans are dry, place them in a large bowl. Add the remaining ingredients, toss, and serve cold.

GREEN BEAN SALAD

1 pound young green beans, rinsed, ends and strings trimmed
1 medium Bermuda onion, seeded and finely shredded
1 medium red bell pepper, seeded and finely shredded
1 clove garlic, crushed
Juice of 1 lemon
½ teaspoon crushed red pepper
1 tablespoon extra-virgin olive oil
½ teaspoon coarsely ground black pepper

♥ POACHED LOBSTER IN BELL PEPPER AND SAFFRON BROTH ♥

The broth in this recipe is essentially a spin-off of court-bouillon, an aromatic liquid acidulated with lemon, wine, or vinegar and used for cooking fish, meat, and vegetables. It is used here as a vehicle for infusing lobster with the flavors of saffron and bell peppers.

4 SERVINGS

4 live lobsters, about 2 pounds each
2 tablespoons extra-virgin olive oil
½ teaspoon saffron threads
1 tablespoon whole black peppercorns
1 bay leaf
1 large onion, finely sliced
1 large green bell pepper, seeded and finely
  sliced lengthwise
1 large red bell pepper, seeded and finely
  sliced lengthwise
1 large yellow bell pepper, seeded and
  finely sliced lengthwise
1 gallon Fish Stock (see Index)
Salt and freshly ground black pepper

To kill the lobsters, place a knife on the point of the head between the eyes and push through. Remove the tail and claws; wrap and freeze the heads and bodies for future use in stock or other recipes.

Heat the oil in a large saucepan until almost smoking. Add the saffron and cook until the oil turns yellow. Stir in the peppercorns, bay leaf, and onion. When the onion is clear and tender, add the green, red, and yellow peppers. Sauté for 2 minutes, then pour in the fish stock. Bring the mixture to a rolling boil and cook for 5 minutes.

Add the lobster tails and claws to the stock and simmer for 5 minutes. Remove the lobster from the stock and let cool slightly, then crack the shells and remove the meat. Slice the tails into medallions and arrange on a platter with the claw meat. Adjust the seasoning of the broth with salt and pepper, then drizzle it around the lobster.

♥ CRAB CAKES WITH FRESH TOMATO-POTATO SAUCE ♥

The old-fashioned way of stretching fish in the home kitchen is to combine the flaked flesh with mashed potatoes and form the mixture into cakes. Restaurants, on the other hand, generally add heavy béchamel sauce, or bread crumbs, or both, to bind their fish cakes. Here I have eliminated the need for the fat- and calorie-laden restaurant additions by going back to the basics and combining mashed potatoes with the crab meat. The formed crab cakes are first browned in a minimal amount of oil, then finished in the oven so they don't soak up any excess fat (see photograph on pages 110–111).

In a large bowl, combine the crab meat, green, red, and yellow bell peppers, cayenne pepper, and mashed potatoes; stir just until blended but do not overwork the mixture or the crab meat will become too shredded. Season with a pinch each of salt and pepper.

Spread parchment or wax paper on a flat work surface. Turn the crab meat mixture onto the paper and pat into a 1¼-inch-thick sheet. Cut into cakes with a 2½-inch round pastry cutter. Place the crab cakes on a tray or baking sheet and refrigerate for 1 hour.

Preheat the oven to 375 degrees F.

Heat the oil in a large skillet over moderately high heat. Test the temperature of the oil with a small cube of bread. If the oil bubbles and the bread begins to brown after 3 to 5 seconds, the oil is hot enough. Dust the crab cakes with flour and place in the hot oil. Cook until lightly browned, about 1 minute per side.

Remove the crab cakes from the pan and drain briefly on paper towels. Transfer to a baking sheet and place in the hot oven for 10 minutes, until the crab cakes are firm and heated through.

Serve immediately, with individual bowls of fresh Tomato-Potato Sauce for dipping. Garnish with jalapeño pepper, bell peppers, and tarragon, if desired.

❧

Preheat the oven to 400 degrees F.

Wash the potatoes and prick with a fork. Line a rimmed baking sheet with a layer of salt approximately ⅛ inch thick. Place the potatoes on the sheet and place in the hot oven until tender, about 1 hour.

Remove the potatoes from the oven and split them lengthwise. When cool enough to handle, scoop out the pulp and place in a blender or food processor. Add the remaining ingredients and blend until smooth.

Serve the sauce either warm or chilled.

4 SERVINGS

1 pound lump crab meat, picked over to remove any shell and cartilage
½ medium green bell pepper, seeded and finely chopped
½ medium red bell pepper, seeded and finely chopped
½ medium yellow bell pepper, seeded and finely chopped
Pinch of cayenne pepper
1 cup mashed potatoes, flavored with 1 teaspoon chopped fresh tarragon leaves
¼ cup light vegetable oil
All-purpose flour, for dusting
Salt and freshly ground black pepper
Tomato-Potato Sauce (recipe follows)
Jalapeño pepper and red and yellow bell pepper strips, for garnish (optional)
Fresh tarragon, for garnish (optional)

TOMATO-POTATO SAUCE

2 large Idaho potatoes
Salt, for lining baking sheet
2 large very ripe tomatoes, peeled, seeded, and finely chopped
2 jalapeño peppers, seeded and finely chopped
6 cornichons, drained and finely chopped
2 tablespoons capers, drained and finely chopped
¼ cup finely chopped Bermuda onion
Juice of 2 lemons
¼ cup extra-virgin olive oil
Salt and freshly ground black pepper

The most common edible species of mussel, Mytilus edulis (more commonly known as the blue or edible mussel), is characterized by its blue-black shell. When shopping, select small mussels, as they are the most tender. Mussels must be alive when they are cooked, so always discard any uncooked mussels whose shells are at all open, a sure sign that the animal inside is dead.

4 SERVINGS

1 quart (about 20) mussels
1 tablespoon all-purpose flour
6 large shallots
1 clove garlic, finely chopped
1 bay leaf
1 cup dry white wine
1 tablespoon extra-virgin olive oil
1 teaspoon sugar
4 large ripe tomatoes, peeled, seeded, and diced
2 tablespoons capers, drained
1 tablespoon chopped fresh parsley
Salt and freshly ground black pepper
Garlic Melba Toast (recipe follows)

Preheat the oven to 375 degrees F.

Scrape the shells of the mussels with a knife to remove the beards and any barnacles. In a large pot, stir the flour into 1 gallon of cold water. Submerge the mussels in the water and let soak for 5 minutes. Drain and rinse thoroughly.

Finely chop two of the shallots and place in a large, heavy pot. Add the mussels, garlic, bay leaf, and wine. Cover and cook over very high heat, shaking the pan occasionally, until the mussels open, about 5 minutes. Remove the mussels from the pan and drain.

When the mussels are cool enough to handle, remove the mussel from the shell, cutting away the rubbery "foot." Set the mussels aside and reserve half of the shells for presentation.

Chop the remaining four shallots. In a medium sauté pan, heat the oil over moderately high heat until almost smoking. Add the shallots and cook until glossy, then add the sugar and tomatoes. Cook, stirring, until the tomatoes break apart, then fold in the capers and parsley. Season with salt and pepper to taste.

Place a small spoonful of tomato and caper relish in each shell. Set one mussel in the shell, then top with additional relish.

Divide the mussels among four ovenproof plates. Place the plates in the hot oven and bake until the relish begins to bubble, about 10 minutes.

Serve the warm mussels with Garlic Melba Toast.

Toast the bread on both sides under a broiler. While the toast is still warm, place it on a flat surface, remove the crusts and, using a serrated knife and a sawing motion, cut each slice horizontally into two slices. Each slice should have a toasted and an untoasted side. With a knife, gently scrape away any bits of soft bread. Spread the untoasted sides with garlic and return to the broiler until lightly toasted. Serve immediately or store in an airtight container for up to one week.

GARLIC MELBA TOAST

8 slices country-style bread, about
  1 inch thick
4 cloves garlic, crushed

Cold, tangy gazpacho is the perfect medium for seafood, and in this recipe, I use Dublin Bay prawns, small members of the lobster family that have several regional names, including scampi and langoustine. Although Dublin Bay prawns are similar in size to jumbo shrimp (otherwise known as prawns), they are distinguished in appearance by their long claws. They are also more tender than jumbo shrimp. Nevertheless, if Dublin Bay prawns are unavailable in your area, you can make this soup with jumbo shrimp instead.

4 SERVINGS

1 teaspoon sea salt
4 tablespoons extra-virgin olive oil
8 fresh basil leaves, very finely shredded
1 clove garlic, crushed
Pinch of ground clove
24 Dublin Bay prawns
Shredded arugula, for garnish
Fresh Croutons (see Index)
Gazpacho (recipe follows)

Preheat the oven to 400 degrees F.

In a small bowl, blend the salt, oil, basil, garlic, and clove. Set the mixture aside while cleaning the prawns.

Split the prawns in half lengthwise. Leaving the heads on, remove and discard the head sacs and intestinal veins. Gently lift the tail away from the shell on each halved prawn. Brush the interior of the shell and exterior of the flesh with the seasoned oil.

Arrange the prawns on a baking sheet and transfer to the hot oven. Roast for 4 minutes, until the flesh is firm.

Arrange the prawns on a bed of shredded arugula. Serve with Fresh Croutons and bowls of Gazpacho.

Place the tomatoes, garlic, cucumber, onion, bell pepper, cayenne pepper, cumin, vinegar, and oil in a blender or food processor and purée until the mixture is the consistency of tomato soup. Adjust the seasoning with salt and pepper, cover, and refrigerate for at least 1 hour.

Chill four glass serving bowls in the freezer.

When thoroughly chilled, remove the gazpacho from the refrigerator. Stir, then pour into the prepared bowls. Place one quarter of the squid, crab meat, and mussels in the center of each portion and sprinkle with basil. Serve immediately.

GAZPACHO

4 medium tomatoes, peeled, seeded, and quartered
2 cloves garlic, crushed
1 small cucumber, peeled, seeded, and quartered
½ medium yellow onion, quartered
1 medium green bell pepper, seeded and quartered
Pinch of cayenne pepper
Pinch of cumin
1 teaspoon rice wine vinegar
3 tablespoons extra-virgin olive oil
Salt and freshly ground white pepper
4 ounces cooked squid, cut into rings
4 ounces lump crab meat, picked over to remove any shell and cartilage
½ cup cooked mussels
Minced fresh basil, for garnish

In this recipe, the sweetness of freshwater prawns is intensified by the byriani, a classic Indian vegetarian dish that I have modified. Instead of saffron, which is traditionally used, I have substituted turmeric because I like the lemony taste it lends the rice.

Shell the prawns, leaving the heads intact. Devein and set aside. In a medium bowl, combine the remaining ingredients through the ginger and blend thoroughly. Toss the prawns in the mixture until well coated, then marinate for 1 hour at room temperature.

Preheat the oven to 375 degrees F. Heat the coals in a barbecue grill until ashen. Lay the papadums directly on the oven rack and bake for 2 minutes, until crisp. Keep warm.

Grill the prawns for 2 minutes per side, until pink. Remove from the heat and let rest for several minutes before serving. Divide the prawns among four plates and serve with the Vegetable Byriani on the side. Garnish with cilantro, if desired.

♥

In a large stainless-steel pot, heat the oil over moderately high heat until almost smoking. When hot, add the onion, carrot, bell pepper, garlic, cardamom, cinnamon, cayenne pepper, and turmeric. Sauté until the onion is tender, then add the tomato and cook for 5 minutes, stirring, until the tomato softens. Stir in the rice and cook for 2 minutes, then add the remaining vegetables. When thoroughly combined, pour in the stock. Cover the pan and simmer the mixture for about 20 minutes, until all of the stock has been absorbed. Remove from the heat and let sit, covered, for 5 minutes.

Before serving, remove the cinnamon stick and toss the mixture with a fork to distribute the vegetables evenly in the rice.

4 SERVINGS

12 large freshwater prawns
Juice of 4 lemons
1 tablespoon Oriental sesame oil
1 clove garlic, crushed
1 teaspoon crushed fresh ginger
4 papadums (an Indian flatbread available at Asian markets and some specialty food stores)
Vegetable Byriani (recipe follows)
Chopped cilantro, for garnish (optional)

VEGETABLE BYRIANI

¼ cup light vegetable oil
½ cup finely diced onion
½ cup finely diced carrot
½ cup finely diced green bell pepper
2 cloves garlic, finely chopped
4 cardamom seeds
½ stick cinnamon
¼ teaspoon cayenne pepper
¼ teaspoon ground turmeric
1 tomato, peeled, seeded, and finely diced
2 cups long-grain rice
½ cup finely diced eggplant
½ cup cauliflower florets
½ cup finely diced yellow squash
½ cup finely diced zucchini
4 cups Chicken Stock (see Index)
Salt and freshly ground black pepper

The combination of grapes and seafood in this recipe is a classical gesture, featured, for instance, in sole Véronique, a French dish with a sauce of wine, cream, and white grapes. Although I have specified muscatel grapes here, any sweet, white seedless grape is acceptable. To complement the very delicate taste of the abalone, I have added a touch of saffron to the accompanying sauce. The meat of the red abalone, though delicious, must be tenderized before cooking.

4 SERVINGS

1 pound muscatel grapes, rinsed
4 red abalone
1 teaspoon unsalted butter
Pinch of saffron threads
½ cup dry white wine
1 teaspoon arrowroot
1 tablespoon light vegetable oil
Salt and freshly ground black pepper

Slice the grapes to the approximate thickness of a penny. Place in a bowl and set aside.

Insert a sharp knife between the abalone and the shell, then sever the muscle that attaches the meat to the shell. Trim the green viscera and any dark patches from the flesh. Rinse the abalone and pat dry.

Slice each abalone into 6 thin rounds. Place the slices between sheets of plastic wrap and pound gently with a mallet until the meat softens and the milky juices seep out. Let rest at room temperature for 15 to 20 minutes.

Melt the butter in a heavy stainless-steel saucepan over medium heat until foamy. Drain the grapes, reserving any juice, and add, along with the saffron, to the butter.

Sauté the grapes for 2 to 3 minutes, then stir in half of the wine and any grape juice. Bring the mixture to a rolling boil, reduce the heat to low, and simmer for 4 to 5 minutes.

Stir the arrowroot into the remaining wine until smooth; add to the grape mixture, stirring constantly. Cook, stirring, until the sauce is thick enough to coat the back of a spoon. Keep warm while cooking the abalone.

Dry the abalone slices and season both sides with salt and pepper. Heat the oil until almost smoking in a large stainless-steel skillet over moderately high heat. Add the slices and sauté for about 30 seconds per side; do not overcook or the abalone will be tough.

Remove the slices from the pan and blot with paper towels. Overlap the slices to form a triangle on each of four dinner plates. Spoon some grapes and sauce around the edges of each triangle and serve.

❧ ROASTED SCALLOPS
WITH ITALIAN TOMATOES, POTATOES, AND BASIL ❧

This scallop salad explores different levels of smoothness, from the marshmallowy texture of the cooked mollusks to the creamy flesh of the potatoes. I use sea scallops rather than bay scallops in this recipe because their larger size makes them both easier to slice and less apt to overcook.

In a heavy skillet, heat the oil to almost smoking. Add the scallops and cook for about 2 minutes, stirring frequently, until lightly browned on both sides. Remove from the pan and drain on paper towels.

Cut each tomato into eight round slices and each potato into four round slices. Split the scallops down the middle.

On each of four serving plates, overlap slices of scallop, potato, and tomato, alternating each ingredient, to form a small circle. Sprinkle with the basil and place one fourth of the watercress in the center of each circle. Spoon Grilled Bermuda Onions onto the watercress and serve.

❧

Light a grill or preheat the broiler.

Brush the onion slices with the red pepper oil and sprinkle with black pepper. Grill or broil for a few minutes, until the pepper begins to bubble in the oil on the onion. Remove from the heat and place in a medium bowl. Separate into rings and toss with the vinegar, sugar, basil, and garlic.

Serve warm.

4 SERVINGS

2 tablespoons extra-virgin olive oil
8 large sea scallops
2 very ripe vine-ripened tomatoes, stemmed
4 yellow-fleshed potatoes, such as yellow Finnish, cooked in their jackets (any small new potatoes can be substituted)
6 fresh basil leaves, finely shredded
1 bunch watercress, washed, stemmed, and quartered
Salt and freshly ground black pepper
Grilled Bermuda Onions with Black Pepper (recipe follows)

GRILLED BERMUDA ONIONS WITH BLACK PEPPER

2 large Bermuda onions, peeled and cut into ½-inch slices
Red Pepper Oil, for brushing (see Index)
Crushed black pepper
2 tablespoons balsamic vinegar
Pinch of brown sugar
1 teaspoon shredded fresh basil
1 clove garlic, crushed

The term urchin originally meant hedgehog, which is exactly what the bristly sea urchin resembles. Its "quills" are needle sharp, so it is necessary to wear protective gloves or use a thick cloth when cleaning the spiny marine animal. This relative of the starfish has a slightly salty flavor and a delicate smoothness that make it a wonderful raw hors d'oeuvre.

4 SERVINGS AS AN APPETIZER

Juice of 6 lemons
1 tablespoon honey
1 teaspoon wasabi powder (available at
    Asian markets)
24 sea urchins
Garlic Melba Toast (see Index)

In a small bowl, combine the lemon juice, honey, and wasabi. Blend thoroughly and let sit at room temperature while preparing the sea urchins.

Turn the sea urchins upside down to access the edible portion, and cut around the mouth with a pair of strong scissors. Separate the dark intestines from the roe sacks and discard. Leave any five-branch roe or milt attached.

Place the opened sea urchins on crushed ice, drizzle with the lemon-honey sauce, and serve with hot Garlic Melba Toast.

Since squid is so popular in the Mediterranean, it is only fitting that it be paired with the Italian eggplant dish called caponata.

This recipe for caponata was passed on to me by a good friend of Italian descent who learned to make it from his mother. You could say that her cooking talents are reflected in the mountainous size of her sons. Use baby squid in this dish, as they are the most tender.

4 SERVINGS

12 baby squid
1 tablespoon extra-virgin olive oil
1 shallot, finely chopped
1 clove garlic, finely chopped
¼ cup dry white wine
Salt and freshly ground black pepper
Caponata (recipe follows)
Fresh basil, for garnish (optional)

Separate the body of the squid from the head and tentacles with a firm tug and a twist. Cut the tentacles from the head, just below the eyes, and cut out the hard "beak." Set the tentacles aside. Discard the head.

Pull off the skin from the body and side fins. Pull out and discard the clear "pen" from the body sac. Cut the fins from the body and turn the sac inside out. Rinse thoroughly with cold water, drain, and pat dry. Cut the body and fins into rings about ¼ inch wide. Season the rings and tentacles with salt and pepper.

❦ *S h e l l f i s h* ❦

Heat the oil in a heavy skillet. When the oil is hot, place the shallots, garlic, and squid in the pan and sauté for about 1 minute. Pour in the wine and cook for another minute. Remove from the heat and let cool, then drain the squid and discard the cooking juices.

Place individual portions of squid in small dishes. Serve the squid either hot or cold, with thick slices of crusty brown bread and small dishes of Caponata on the side. Garnish with fresh basil, if desired.

❦

Preheat the oven to 400 degrees F.

Spread the pine nuts in a single layer in a pie pan. Roast in the hot oven until golden brown, about 5 minutes. Remove from the oven and let cool completely.

Heat 2 tablespoons of the oil in a heavy saucepan over moderately high heat. When the oil is hot, add the tomatoes, onion, garlic, and Italian seasoning. Simmer for about 15 minutes over low heat, then remove from the heat and set aside.

Place the eggplant in a bowl or colander and sprinkle with salt. Let sit at room temperature for 20 minutes, then rinse thoroughly under cold running water and drain on paper towels.

Heat the remaining oil in a skillet until it begins to sizzle, then sauté the eggplant until tender, about 3 to 4 minutes. Fold in the pine nuts, then remove from the heat and let cool.

Blanch the celery and olives in boiling water for 1 to 2 minutes. Immerse in cold water, drain, and blot dry with paper towels. Fold the celery, olives, and eggplant mixture into the tomato mixture.

Combine the vinegar, sugar, and 2 tablespoons water in a small saucepan. Cook over medium heat until the sugar dissolves, about 3 minutes. Remove from the heat and let cool.

Gradually stir the vinegar mixture into the eggplant. Season with salt and pepper, then cover and refrigerate. Serve the Caponata chilled.

CAPONATA

½ cup pine nuts
¼ cup extra-virgin olive oil
2 very ripe medium tomatoes, peeled, seeded, and chopped
¼ cup peeled and finely chopped onion
1 teaspoon minced garlic
Pinch of Italian seasoning
½ medium eggplant, peeled and finely chopped
2 ribs celery, finely chopped
½ cup pitted green olives, drained and finely chopped
2 tablespoons red wine vinegar
2 tablespoons sugar
Salt and freshly ground black pepper

Depending on your appetite and the occasion, the following recipes can be executed separately or can be combined and served as a single dish.

BABY SQUID

4 SERVINGS

16 baby squid
1 tablespoon Roasted Garlic Purée
   (see Index)
1 tablespoon finely chopped flat-leaf
   parsley
1 tablespoon plus 1 teaspoon extra-virgin
   olive oil
Salt and freshly ground black pepper

Remove the eyes and hard "beak" from each squid. Make an incision behind the head and pull out the clear "pen" from the pouch; do not separate the body from the head. Wash thoroughly and drain.

In a small bowl, blend the garlic purée, parsley, and 1 teaspoon of the olive oil.

Spoon about ¼ teaspoon of the garlic mixture into each body sac. Season the squid with salt and pepper, and toss in 1 tablespoon of the olive oil.

Preheat a griddle or shallow cast-iron frying pan until drops of cold water sprinkled on it form beads that pop and bounce. Cook the squid on the griddle or in the pan for about 1 minute. Turn and cook for another minute until fairly tender.

Serve each person four warm baby squid on a bed of Wilted Arugula.

In a small bowl, blend the garlic purée, parsley, and 1 teaspoon of olive oil.

Split the langoustines down the middle on the backside and pull the raw tail meat out of the shell; leave the heads and claws attached. Rub the insides of the shells with the garlic mixture. Return the tail meat to the shell and brush lightly with oil.

Preheat a griddle or shallow cast-iron frying pan until drops of cold water sprinkled on it form beads that pop and bounce. Cook the langoustines, meat side down, on the griddle or in the pan for about 1 minute, until the flesh turns pink. Turn and cook for another minute.

Serve each person four warm langoustines on a bed of Wilted Arugula.

Note: Langoustines are shrimp-size members of the lobster family. In some regions, they are known as scampi or Dublin Bay prawns.

❧

In a large bowl, toss the arugula with the vinegar. Upon serving, the heat from the seafood will wilt the arugula.

LANGOUSTINES

4 SERVINGS

1 tablespoon Roasted Garlic Purée
    (see Index)
1 tablespoon finely chopped flat-leaf
    parsley
1 teaspoon extra-virgin olive oil, plus more
    for brushing on the langoustines
16 large fresh (not frozen) langoustines
    (see Note)
Wilted Arugula (recipe follows)

WILTED ARUGULA

1 bunch arugula, large stems removed
1 tablespoon red wine vinegar

Freshly caught trout

3

The
Freshwater
System

❦ BROWN TROUT IN BRIOCHE CRUMBS
WITH DILL AND PARMESAN ❦

The key ingredient in the following recipe is the brioche, which can be purchased at most French bakeries. The rich, buttery flavor of the bread combines extremely well with the earthiness of the trout, and the featherlight crumbs fry up crispier than ordinary bread crumbs.

Preheat the oven to 375 degrees F.

Combine the oil and rosemary in a small saucepan. Simmer for 1 to 2 minutes over very low heat, until the rosemary releases its aroma. Strain the oil into a heavy skillet and set aside; discard the rosemary.

In a shallow bowl, combine the brioche crumbs, dill, and Parmesan.

Season the trout fillets on both sides with salt and pepper, then dip in the egg whites. Press both sides of the fillets firmly into the brioche mixture.

Heat the rosemary-flavored olive oil over moderately high heat until it begins to sizzle. Brown the fillets in the hot oil, about 30 seconds per side. Remove the fish from the skillet and blot on paper towels. Transfer the fillets to a baking sheet and place in the hot oven for 5 minutes.

Serve the warm brown trout with Sun-Dried Tomato and Celery Salad on the side.

❧

In a small bowl, toss the sun-dried tomato and celery in the vinegar. Sprinkle with chives and pepper, and serve.

4 SERVINGS

1 tablespoon extra-virgin olive oil
½ teaspoon finely chopped fresh
    rosemary leaves
¾ cup sieved brioche crumbs
1 tablespoon finely chopped fresh dill
1 tablespoon freshly grated Parmesan
    cheese
8 skinless brown trout fillets, about
    5 ounces each
2 egg whites, beaten until frothy
Salt and freshly ground black pepper
Sun-Dried Tomato and Celery Salad
    (recipe follows)

SUN-DRIED TOMATO AND CELERY SALAD

2 oil-packed sun-dried tomatoes,
    finely sliced
2 ribs celery, stringy fibers scraped away,
    finely shredded
2 tablespoons apple cider vinegar
1 tablespoon chopped fresh chives
Cracked black pepper, for sprinkling

The challenge I faced when developing this dish was how to impart a smoked flavor to the sturgeon without macerating it in so much sugar and salt that the fish was actually cured, as for Swedish gravlax. The brief marination of the sturgeon in small quantities of salt, sugar, and dill is a light cure that does not preclude cooking. Similarly, during the brief period of smoking stipulated here smoke does not penetrate (cook) the fish, but rather imparts flavor to the exterior layer of the fish. What the one-two punch of curing and smoking does is lock in the moisture of the sturgeon and ultimately shorten the cooking time normally required for this dense fish.

Combine the salt, sugar, and ¼ cup dill in a small bowl. Place the sturgeon fillets on a rimmed baking sheet or tray. Press the salt mixture onto both sides of the sturgeon. Let sit for 20 minutes at room temperature, then rinse the fillets for 10 minutes under cold running water. Pat dry with paper towels.

Preheat a smoker according to the manufacturer's instructions, using the oak or hickory chips. When the smoker is hot, place the fish fillets inside and cook for 15 minutes. Remove the fillets and allow to cool.

Boil the potatoes in salted water until tender enough to pierce easily with a fork, about 15 minutes. Do not overcook. Drain the potatoes and, while still hot, dice into a bowl. Add the onion, the remaining teaspoon of dill, and the yogurt. Season with salt and pepper. Stir just until the chunks of potato are coated with the yogurt.

Slice each sturgeon fillet into four pieces. Melt the butter in a large, heavy skillet, then add the sturgeon and cook over moderate heat for about 5 minutes, turning once about halfway through. Remove from the pan and drain on paper towels.

Fan four slices of sturgeon on each plate. Serve potato salad garnished with caviar on the side. If desired, garnish with red and yellow bell pepper and dill.

4 SERVINGS

¼ cup salt
¼ cup sugar
¼ cup plus 1 teaspoon chopped fresh dill
4 sturgeon fillets, about 8 ounces each
Oak or hickory chips, for smoking
1 pound small yellow Finnish potatoes, jackets scrubbed (red bliss or small new potatoes may be substituted)
½ Vidalia onion, finely chopped (any mild, sweet onion may be substituted)
4 tablespoons plain yogurt
¼ cup (½ stick) unsalted butter
1 ounce (2 tablespoons) Beluga caviar
Salt and freshly ground black pepper
Red and yellow bell pepper strips, for garnish (optional)
Fresh dill, for garnish (optional)

This recipe relies upon the multicultural tradition of curing fish with vine-gar or wine plus oil and spices. More specifically, this version pays homage to harengs au Riesling, a German dish adapted by the French, in which herrings are marinated in a wine-based sauce.

4 SERVINGS AS AN APPETIZER

4 baby coho salmon, butterfly filleted
   (about 8 ounces each), cleaned, head
   and tail removed
2 cups Riesling wine
¼ cup extra-virgin olive oil
½ Vidalia onion, finely sliced (any mild,
   sweet onion may be substituted)
1 carrot, finely shredded
1 leek, white part only, finely shredded
1 teaspoon crushed juniper berries
Pinch of salt
½ teaspoon crushed black pepper
1 cup bean sprouts, for garnish

Spread open the stomach cavity of the salmon and place, flesh side up, in a shallow dish. In a medium saucepan, combine the remaining ingredients through the black pepper. Bring the mixture to a boil, stirring continuously. Boil for 2 minutes, then remove from the heat and whisk rapidly until the mixture begins to emulsify. Pour the mixture over the salmon and let sit at room temperature until cool. Cover with plastic wrap and refrigerate for 24 hours.

Remove the fish from the marinade and serve cold as an appetizer, accompanied by vegetables from the marinade. Garnish each plate with bean sprouts.

❧ *The Freshwater System* ❧

This is a faithful rendition of the venerable French truite au bleu. A surprising chemical reaction between vinegar and the natural coating of the fish actually transforms rainbow trout from blue-hued to sky blue during the cooking process. Of course, this is assuming you have access to live trout; fresh (but already killed) fish turn out just as tasty using this method, but the results are not nearly as dramatic.

Fill a stockpot with 1 gallon water. Add the wine, carrot, leek, bay leaves, peppercorns, and salt, and bring to a rolling boil. Simmer, uncovered, for 15 minutes.

Five minutes before you plan to cook the fish, kill the trout with a blow to the head. Clean and gut the fish as quickly as possible, then arrange them in a single layer in a shallow dish. Pour the vinegar over the fish, making sure they are well coated.

Holding the trout by their tails, turn the fish and coat the other side; let sit in the vinegar for 1 minute, then immerse in the simmering stock. As soon as the fish turn blue, remove the pot from the heat and let the fish steep in the stock for 2 minutes.

Remove the trout with a slotted spoon and set atop portions of Braised Red Cabbage. Serve Clove-Boiled Potatoes on the side.

4 SERVINGS

2 cups dry white wine
1 carrot, thinly sliced
1 leek, white and green parts, thinly
    sliced crosswise
2 bay leaves
1 tablespoon whole white peppercorns
1 tablespoon salt
4 live rainbow trout
½ cup champagne vinegar
Braised Red Cabbage (recipe follows)
Clove-Boiled Potatoes (see Index)

❦

Preheat the oven to 375 degrees F.

In a large casserole dish, combine the cabbage, onion, bay leaf, nutmeg, and vinegar. Season with salt and pepper. Cover and braise in the hot oven for 1 hour.

Stir in the apples and sugar, and return to the oven until the cabbage is tender, approximately 30 minutes. Serve warm.

BRAISED RED CABBAGE

1 pound red cabbage, finely shredded
1 large white onion, finely shredded
1 bay leaf
Pinch of nutmeg
1 tablespoon red wine vinegar
2 Granny Smith apples, peeled and
    shredded
1 tablespoon brown sugar
Salt and freshly ground black pepper

When rainbow trout were available strictly through the efforts of anglers, these sweet, mild fish were considered a luxury. Modern aquaculture has made the delicate freshwater fish more accessible and has thus inspired culinary experimentation like this combination of rainbow trout and pan- or griddle-fried jalapeño corn fritters. For best results, don't overcook the fritters.

4 SERVINGS

4 whole rainbow trout (8 to 10 ounces each), cleaned
¼ cup lemon juice
1 tablespoon plus 1 teaspoon extra-virgin olive oil
¼ teaspoon freshly ground black pepper
1 cup milk
2 ears sweet corn, shucked
1 jalapeño pepper, seeded and finely chopped
2 shallots, finely chopped
2 egg whites
½ cup sifted all-purpose flour
Pinch of baking powder
Light vegetable oil, for brushing

With a sharp knife, score the trout four times on each side. In a small bowl, combine the lemon juice, 1 tablespoon olive oil, and the black pepper. Rub this mixture inside the trout and on the skin. Place the trout in a glass dish, cover, and refrigerate.

Combine the milk with 2 cups water in a large saucepan and bring the mixture to a boil. Place the corn in the pan and reduce the heat. Simmer for 12 minutes, covered, until the corn is tender. Remove the ears of corn from the pan and drain on paper towels. When cool enough to handle, scrape the kernels off the cobs with a sharp knife. Place the kernels in a bowl and set aside.

In a small sauté pan, heat 1 teaspoon olive oil over moderately high heat until it starts to release its aroma. Add the jalapeño peppers and shallots, and sauté in the hot oil until the shallots are translucent; remove from the heat and let cool.

In a stainless-steel bowl, beat the egg whites until they form stiff peaks. Gently fold in the corn kernels, jalapeño peppers, shallots, flour, and baking powder, working quickly so as not to deflate the egg whites.

Heat a skillet or griddle over moderately high heat until a drop of water sizzles and pops upon contact, then brush lightly with vegetable oil. Spoon tablespoons of batter into the hot pan. Brown the first side, 2 to 3 minutes, then turn and brown the other side. Keep the fritters warm until serving.

Preheat a grill.

Cook the trout in the center of the hot grill for about 5 minutes on each side, turning only once, until flaky and opaque. Watch carefully to avoid burning the fish. Transfer the trout to four plates and serve with the warm corn fritters.

I love the texture of salmon. The flesh has a muscled grain that seems to slide rather than break apart. Unfortunately, salmon is frequently paired with heavy sauces that mask the character of the fish. The potato vinaigrette in this dish is similar to mayonnaise in consistency but contains no fat.

In a small saucepan, warm the red wine vinegar. Add the brown sugar and cook over low heat, stirring, until the sugar dissolves. Remove from the heat and let cool.

Pour the vinegar mixture into a shallow dish that is large enough to accommodate all four salmon fillets. Place the fillets in the dish, flesh side down, and marinate at room temperature for 20 minutes.

Preheat the oven to 375 degrees F.

Remove the salmon from the marinade and drain on paper towels. In a large, heavy, ovenproof skillet, heat the oil over moderately high heat until almost smoking. Criscross two rosemary sprigs on the fleshy side of each fillet, then place each fillet, rosemary side down, in the hot pan. Sear over high heat for 2 minutes, then turn and cook the other side for 2 minutes.

Cover the skillet with aluminum foil and place in the hot oven for about 3 minutes, until the fish flakes when tested with a fork. Remove the salmon from the skillet and drain on paper towels.

Spoon a couple of tablespoons of Potato Vinaigrette onto the center of four serving plates. Set a salmon fillet in the vinaigrette and serve.

4 SERVINGS

½ cup red wine vinegar

¼ cup light brown sugar (preferably West Indian Demerara brown sugar)

4 salmon fillets, with skin, about 6 ounces each

2 tablespoons extra-virgin olive oil

8 sprigs rosemary, approximately 4 inches in length

Potato Vinaigrette (recipe follows)

❤

In a medium saucepan, combine 2 cups chicken stock, the potato, thyme, and garlic. Bring to a boil and cook until the potato is tender, about 15 minutes. Transfer to a blender and purée. Add the vinegar, oil, and salt and pepper to taste. Dilute with additional chicken stock if the consistency seems too thick. The vinaigrette can be made ahead and refrigerated. Serve cold or at room temperature.

Leftover vinaigrette can be served with cooked shrimp, crab meat, mussels, or scallops on a bed of lettuce or wilted greens. It will keep for up to 7 to 10 days.

POTATO VINAIGRETTE

2 or more cups Chicken Stock (see Index)

1 large baking potato (about ½ pound), peeled and diced

Pinch of fresh thyme leaves

1 clove garlic

3 tablespoons champagne vinegar

2 tablespoons extra-virgin olive oil

Salt and freshly ground black pepper

❦ TILAPIA WITH CITRUS AND THREE PEPPERS ❦

This ancient fish is originally from Africa and was even depicted in Egyptian hieroglyphics. Adaptable to either fresh or salt water, this member of the cichlid family is now cultivated around the world, and is rapidly gaining new fans who favor its moist white flesh and versatility.

4 SERVINGS

4 skinless tilapia fillets, about 6 ounces each
¼ cup cornstarch
2 egg whites, beaten until frothy
¼ cup canola oil
1 tablespoon Red Pepper Oil (see Index)
1 green bell pepper, seeded and finely julienned
1 red bell pepper, seeded and finely julienned
1 yellow bell pepper, seeded and finely julienned
1 orange, peeled and segmented
1 lemon, peeled and segmented
1 teaspoon chopped fresh cilantro
Salt and freshly ground black pepper

Season the tilapia on both sides with salt and pepper. Dust the fillets with cornstarch and dip in the egg whites.

In a heavy skillet, heat the canola oil over moderately high heat until almost smoking. Add the fillets and sauté in the hot oil until brown and crispy, 1 to 2 minutes per side. Remove the fillets from the pan and drain on paper towels. Keep warm until serving.

In another skillet, heat the red pepper oil over moderately high heat until it begins to sizzle. Add the green, red, and yellow bell peppers, and cook over high heat for approximately 1 minute. Stir in the orange and lemon segments, and sauté for another minute. Remove from the heat and sprinkle with cilantro.

In the center of each of four plates, mound a bed of citrus and peppers; top with a tilapia fillet and serve.

❦ BROILED CATFISH WITH HORSERADISH AND ORANGE ZEST ❦

Since these fish take on the taste of the water in which they live, I always use farm-raised catfish. Modern cultivation methods ensure fish that are cleaner than the ones pulled out of muddy rivers and streams.

4 SERVINGS

2 tablespoons canola oil
1 very ripe tomato
1 teaspoon Creole mustard
1 tablespoon champagne vinegar
1 clove garlic
¼ cup freshly grated horseradish
1 tablespoon grated and blanched orange zest (see Note)

In a blender or food processor, combine the oil, tomato, mustard, vinegar, and garlic. Purée mixture, then strain through a fine sieve. Refrigerate until ready to use.

Mix the horseradish, orange zest, peppercorns, and scallions in a small bowl. Set the mixture aside.

Preheat the broiler.

Season the catfish fillets on both sides with salt and pepper. Place the fillets on a baking sheet and broil for 2 minutes. Turn the fillets and cook for an additional 2 minutes, until flaky and opaque.

Remove the fish from the broiler and let rest for 2 minutes. Nap serving plates with cold tomato-mustard sauce. Set a catfish fillet in the center of each plate, dot with the horseradish mixture, and serve.

Note: Blanching tenderizes the orange zest and removes any bitterness. To blanch, drop the grated zest into boiling water for a few seconds, then drain in a fine-meshed sieve.

¼ teaspoon ground pink peppercorns
2 scallions, finely shredded
4 skinless catfish fillets, about 8 ounces each
Salt and freshly ground black pepper

❦ TEMPURA OF CARP WITH VINEGARED PINEAPPLE ❦

The key to the crisp coating of Japanese tempura is timing. Although the batter is simplicity itself, it must be prepared at the last minute before cooking (see photograph on following pages).

With a sharp knife, cut the carp fillet on the diagonal into ¼-inch-wide strips.

In a medium bowl, combine the sesame seeds, ginger, star anise, garlic, cayenne pepper, salt, and pepper. Toss the strips of carp in the sesame seed mixture. Spread the carp on a tray, cover with plastic wrap, and refrigerate for 2 hours.

Arrange the sliced pineapple to cover the base of four serving plates. Sprinkle the slices with vinegar and cilantro, and set aside.

Heat the oil in a deep-fat fryer or large saucepan to 365 degrees F. Near the fryer, position a cloth-lined tray for draining the cooked fish.

Beat the egg with the ice water in a stainless-steel bowl. Add the flour and stir just until moistened; the batter will still be slightly lumpy.

Coat the carp strips with a thin film of batter. Fry in batches in the hot oil for about 1 minute, until the strips float to the surface and the batter is crispy. Drain and serve immediately on the pineapple slices.

4 SERVINGS

2 pounds skinned carp fillet
2 teaspoons sesame seeds
½ teaspoon finely chopped fresh ginger
1 teaspoon ground star anise
1 clove garlic, very finely chopped
¼ teaspoon cayenne pepper
½ teaspoon salt
½ teaspoon freshly ground black pepper
1 ripe pineapple, peeled, cored, and thinly sliced
4 tablespoons rice wine vinegar
1 tablespoon chopped fresh cilantro
1 quart (4 cups) peanut oil
1 large egg
1½ cups ice water
2½ cups all-purpose flour

The European and American freshwater eels are well-traveled fish that spawn in the Sargasso Sea in the western Atlantic. From there the young eels swim long distances to their home waters around the world. Eel has been fished and eaten in Europe since medieval times, and jellied eel is still popular in the south of England today. When cooked, the snakelike creature produces a natural jelly that makes the introduction of animal gelatins into this dish unnecessary. Although eel is a great source of protein, dishes featuring eel are for many people more of a curiosity than anything else; I, therefore, prefer to appoint them to the appetizer course.

8 SERVINGS AS AN APPETIZER

3 large live eels, about 2 pounds
Salt, for skinning
½ cup vinegar
½ cup dry white wine
1 onion, finely diced
½ teaspoon coarse (kosher) salt
¼ teaspoon ground white pepper
1 whole clove
¼ teaspoon finely chopped fresh thyme
¼ teaspoon finely chopped fresh rosemary
¼ teaspoon finely chopped fresh sage
¼ teaspoon finely chopped fresh basil
¼ teaspoon finely chopped fresh marjoram
16 Belgian endive leaves, for garnish
1 small ripe tomato, diced, for garnish
½ red bell pepper, seeded and diced, for garnish
½ yellow bell pepper, seeded and diced, for garnish
Fresh sorrel and dill, for garnish (optional)

Preheat the oven to 375 degrees F.

Just before skinning the eels, kill them either with a sharp blow to the head or by piercing the spinal cord with a knife. Rub the eel with salt to facilitate handling, then make a slit in the skin about 3 inches below the head, all the way around the eel. Cut the skin loose, then, using pliers if necessary, peel the skin from the head to the tail, stripping it downward.

Slit the eel on the belly side and remove and discard the gut. Rinse thoroughly, then cut each eel into four equal pieces. Place the eel, the remaining ingredients through the marjoram, and 2 cups cold water in a large casserole. Bring the mixture to a boil over high heat.

Cover and transfer to the hot oven. Poach until the meat of the eel falls off the bone, about 1 hour. Remove the pieces of eel from the baking dish and let cool. Strain the stock from the casserole into a stainless-steel saucepan and reduce by half over medium heat.

Pick the eel meat from the bone and divide the pieces among eight ½-cup ramekins or molds. Cover the eel with the reduced stock and let cool. Cover with plastic wrap and refrigerate overnight.

Before serving, dip the bottoms of the molds in hot water and invert onto small plates. Garnish each plate with 2 endive leaves filled with diced tomato and diced red and yellow bell pepper. Garnish with sorrel and dill, if desired.

The roots of this dish are completely North American—from the striped bass, which was a staple of the early settlers in New England, to the potato, which was first cultivated in the New World.

4 SERVINGS

12 striped bass fillets, 3 to 4 ounces each
¼ cup extra-virgin olive oil
4 teaspoons balsamic vinegar
Salt and freshly ground black pepper
Dill Mashed Potatoes (recipe follows)

Preheat the oven to 375 degrees F.

Season the fillets on both sides with salt and pepper.

Heat the oil in a large ovenproof skillet over moderately high heat until almost smoking. Sear the fish in the hot oil, about 1 minute per side, then transfer to the oven and bake until fully cooked, 10 to 12 minutes. Remove the bass from the pan and drain on paper towels.

Brush each bass with the vinegar and serve with Dill Mashed Potatoes.

Preheat the oven to 400 degrees F.

Wash the potatoes and prick with a fork. Line a rimmed baking sheet with a layer of salt approximately ⅛ inch thick. Place the potatoes on the sheet and place in the hot oven until tender, about 1 hour.

Remove the potatoes from the oven and split lengthwise. When cool enough to handle, scoop out the pulp and place in a bowl. Add the remaining ingredients and mash with a fork. Serve warm.

DILL MASHED POTATOES

4 large Idaho potatoes
Salt, for lining baking sheet
1 tablespoon chopped fresh dill leaves
2 tablespoons extra-virgin olive oil
Salt and freshly ground black pepper

❧ PIKE IN ONION AND GARLIC CRUST ❧

This ominous-looking predator is characterized by razor-sharp teeth and a plethora of fine bones. Careful filleting, however, yields a silver lining— the slightly sweet flesh of the freshwater pike.

Preheat the oven to 375 degrees F.

In a heavy skillet, heat the oil over moderately high heat until almost smoking. Add the garlic and onion and sauté until crisp and golden brown, about 5 minutes. Remove the mixture from the heat and drain in a fine sieve, reserving the oil in one small bowl and the garlic and onions in another small bowl.

Before scaling the pike, remove any mucus by dousing the fish in boiling water. The substance will coagulate and can then be rinsed off. Scrape away all the scales, then gut the fish. Remove the gills, head, and tail.

To fillet the pike, insert a sharp knife inside the belly cavity at the point where the head was attached to the fish. Run the knife along the spine and cut the fish open so that it lays flat; be careful not to cut the fish in half.

Open the fish and remove the ribs by cutting up into the bone, with the knife laid against the flesh.

4 SERVINGS

¼ cup extra-virgin olive oil
20 cloves garlic, finely chopped
1 large white onion, finely chopped
1 whole pike, about 6 pounds
1 teaspoon finely chopped fresh
    marjoram leaves
1 teaspoon finely chopped fresh
    thyme leaves
Salt and freshly ground black pepper
Hot Grilled Tomatoes with Rice Vinegar
    and Mint (recipe follows)

(continued on next page)

When all the bones have been removed, sprinkle the opened fish with the marjoram, thyme, salt, and pepper. Spread the garlic and onion mixture over the flesh, then place the two sides together to close and re-form the fish.

Place the fish on a rimmed baking sheet and brush the skin with the reserved oil. Transfer to the hot oven and roast for 35 minutes; baste occasionally with the pan drippings.

Remove the pan from the oven and let the fish sit for approximately 10 minutes before removing the skin. Pull the skin off the top fillet first, starting at the corner where the gill flap was located. Repeat the process with the bottom fillet.

Cut each fillet into two pieces and serve with Hot Grilled Tomatoes with Rice Vinegar and Mint on the side.

❦

HOT GRILLED TOMATOES WITH RICE VINEGAR AND MINT

2 teaspoons finely chopped mint leaves
¼ teaspoon sugar
4 tablespoons rice wine vinegar
4 large ripe tomatoes

In a small bowl, combine the mint with the sugar. Add the vinegar and toss. Set the mixture aside.

Preheat the broiler.

Cut the tomatoes into very thin slices. Arrange a single layer of tomato on four ovenproof plates, 10 inches in diameter. Shingle, or overlap, the slices to cover each plate. Place the plates under the broiler for 1 minute.

Remove the plates from the broiler, sprinkle with the rice vinegar–mint dressing, and serve immediately.

About 15,000 years ago when the ice sheet started to retreat, the entire complexion of the Northern Hemisphere changed: Land masses tilted, the sea level rose, and rivers rerouted. The topographical upheaval created physical boundaries that isolated some fish in inland waters. Today, one species of char inhabits cold-water seas and another type can be found in landlocked fresh water, which indicates to me that it is a very old fish indeed. For preparation of this intriguing fish, I chose the court-bouillon, a time-honored aromatic broth used for poaching delicate fish, vegetables, and veal.

Fill a large stainless-steel stockpot with 1 gallon water. Add the wine, carrot, leek, bay leaves, peppercorns, and salt. Bring the stock to a rolling boil. Simmer, uncovered, for 15 minutes. Place the char in the court-bouillon and simmer for 5 minutes. Remove the pot from the heat and cool the contents until the liquid is warm but not hot. Carefully remove the char from the pot with a large slotted spoon and place on a work surface.

Peel away the skin from the head to the tail. Draw a sharp knife down the lateral line (the line running along the side of the body from the head to the tail) and gently separate the top fillet from the bone and separate into two portions. Sever the spine at the base of the head and at the tail, and ease out the backbone. Remove the head and discard. Remove any remaining bones from the two bottom fillet portions.

Place the two fish side by side on a platter. Fill the backbone cavity of the bottom fillets on each char with Tomato Vinaigrette and cover with the top fillets, creating a sandwich. Serve immediately.

♥

Core the tomatoes and coarsely chop them. In a blender, combine the chopped tomatoes, garlic, oil, and vinegar. Blend at high speed until smooth. Fold in the sage, then season with salt and pepper to taste. Refrigerate until ready to use.

4 SERVINGS

2 cups dry white wine
1 carrot, thinly sliced
1 leek, white and green parts, thinly
    sliced crosswise
2 bay leaves
1 tablespoon whole white peppercorns
1 tablespoon salt
2 char (about 2 pounds each), cleaned
Tomato Vinaigrette with Sage
    (recipe follows)

TOMATO VINAIGRETTE
WITH SAGE

4 large, very ripe tomatoes
½ teaspoon Roasted Garlic Purée
    (see Index)
1 cup extra-virgin olive oil
½ cup balsamic vinegar
1 teaspoon finely chopped fresh sage leaves
Salt and freshly ground black pepper

4

Stocks,
Seasonings,
& Seafood
Combinations

As chefs discovered centuries ago, salmon and caviar are a perfect marriage of taste and texture. Instead of smoking or curing the salmon, which is how it was handled historically, I sear the fish quickly to lock in its flavor. In order to maintain the integrity of the caviar, however, it is imperative not to allow the roe to cook. The yogurt sauce with lavender blossoms provides a Middle Eastern bent to the dish. If you prefer, substitute any flowering herb for the lavender. The finished dish is shown in the photograph on the preceding pages.

4 SERVINGS

1 pound salmon fillet, middle-cut, about
   1 inch thick
4 ounces (½ cup) Beluga caviar
1 tablespoon chopped fresh chives
Dash of Hungarian paprika
2 tablespoons unsalted butter
1 shallot, finely chopped
¼ teaspoon dried lavender blossoms
   (available at Middle Eastern markets
   and some specialty food stores)
2 tablespoons plain yogurt
1 teaspoon lemon juice
¼ cup champagne
1 teaspoon canola oil
Fresh chives, for garnish (optional)

Slice the salmon into four pieces, about 4 ounces each. Place the pieces between sheets of plastic wrap and pound gently to a thickness of about ⅛ inch.

Mound caviar in the center of each slice of salmon. Sprinkle the caviar with the chives and paprika. Fold the salmon over the caviar and press the edges to seal the pocket.

Melt the butter in a small sauté pan. Add the shallot and lavender, and cook over low heat until the shallot is tender; do not allow the mixture to burn. Remove from the heat and let cool.

In a small bowl, combine the yogurt, lemon juice, and cooled shallot mixture, then fold in the champagne. Cover the bowl and refrigerate for 30 minutes or until ready to use.

Heat a heavy skillet and coat the bottom with a thin film of canola oil. Sear each salmon pocket in the hot pan, about 15 seconds per side, to medium-rare.

Nap the cold yogurt sauce on serving plates and place a salmon pocket in the center of each plate in the pool of sauce. Garnish with chives, if desired.

Paysanne, which in culinary terms means "thinly sliced," refers to the cut of the floating garnish for this soup, which can be served either hot or cold. This rich consommé is a delicious use for lobster remains from recipes that call for only the meat of the shellfish.

Place the lobster heads and carcasses, onion, roughly chopped leek, roughly chopped celery, tomatoes, saffron, and cardamom seeds in a stockpot. Add the egg whites and wine, and whisk the mixture until frothy. Pour in the fish stock and place over high heat. Do not stir.

As soon as a "raft" of vegetables and egg whites forms on top of the stock, lower the heat and simmer gently until the raft cooks and becomes firm to the touch. Strain the stock through a cheesecloth-lined sieve set over a large saucepan and keep warm over low heat. Do not allow to boil. Discard the raft.

To complete preparation of the garnish, cut the carrots in half lengthwise, then in half again. Finely slice the quartered carrot. Scrape the backs of the 2 whole celery ribs to remove any strings, then slice into fine pieces.

Melt the butter in a medium sauté pan and cook the finely sliced carrots, celery, mushrooms, and leeks over low heat until tender, about 15 to 20 minutes. Remove from the pan with a slotted spoon and set aside.

Add the sole strips to the pan and cook until the fish turns white, about 1 minute, turning the fish after 30 seconds. Remove from the pan and combine with the vegetables.

Check the seasoning of the consommé and add salt and pepper to taste. Ladle into bowls and add a tablespoon of the vegetable and sole mixture to each serving.

MAKES ABOUT 2 QUARTS

6 lobster heads and carcasses
1 large white onion, roughly chopped
2 leeks, white part only, 1 roughly chopped, 1 finely sliced
6 ribs celery, 4 roughly chopped, 2 whole
3 very ripe tomatoes, roughly chopped
Pinch of saffron threads
10 cardamom seeds
1 cup (about 6 to 7) egg whites
1 cup dry white wine
3 quarts (12 cups) Fish Stock (see Index)
2 carrots
1 tablespoon unsalted butter
4 shiitake mushrooms, stems discarded and caps finely sliced
4 skinned sole fillets (about 1 ½ to 2 ounces each), cut into ¼-inch strips
Salt and freshly ground white pepper

To *counterbalance the natural sweetness of the shellfish in this hearty dish, I add sorrel, a lemony-flavored member of the buckwheat family. It is incorporated into the seafood mixture just before serving, away from the heat, to preserve its green color. Of the various species of sorrel, Rumex scutatus, or French sorrel, produces the best-tasting leaves.*

In a small bowl, dissolve the arrowroot in the Pernod and set aside.

In a large heavy skillet, heat the oil over moderately high heat until almost smoking. Add the shallots and bay leaf. Sauté for 2 to 3 minutes, then add the mussels and clams. Cover the pan and let steam until the shells open, about 5 to 7 minutes. Add the shrimp, scallops, and crab claws, along with the lobster stock. Bring the mixture to a rolling boil, then reduce the heat and simmer for 3 minutes.

Remove all the shellfish with a slotted spoon and set aside. Reduce the liquid in the pan over low heat for 10 minutes, then stir in the arrowroot mixture. Adjust the seasoning with salt and pepper to taste; cook just until thick enough to coat the back of a spoon, almost 20 minutes. Remove from the heat and return the shellfish to the thickened sauce.

Just before serving, remove the bay leaf, transfer the shellfish and sauce to a soup tureen, and sprinkle with the shredded sorrel. Serve with warm bread and Garlic Spread.

4 SERVINGS

1 teaspoon arrowroot
1 tablespoon Pernod
1 tablespoon extra-virgin olive oil
6 shallots, finely sliced
1 bay leaf
8 mussels, scrubbed and debearded
4 cherrystone clams, scrubbed
4 large shrimp, peeled and deveined
8 sea scallops
4 stone crab claws, cracked
4 cups Lobster Stock (see Index)
Salt and freshly ground black pepper
10 fresh sorrel leaves, finely shredded
Warm bread
Garlic Spread (recipe follows)

❦

Place the ingredients in a blender or small bowl and mix until smooth and well combined.

Use immediately as a spread for warm bread, or cover and store for up to several weeks in the refrigerator.

GARLIC SPREAD

¼ cup Roasted Garlic Purée (see Index)
¼ cup extra-virgin olive oil
½ cup freshly grated Parmesan cheese
1 tablespoon Worcestershire sauce
¼ cup chopped fresh parsley
½ teaspoon chopped fresh basil leaves
½ teaspoon freshly ground black pepper

The following recipe calls for firm white fish, salmon, and tuna, but these are merely suggestions. For variety, try drum or flounder instead of grouper or red snapper; pompano or sea bream instead of salmon; and swordfish or opah instead of tuna. The ingredients for the classic Genoese pesto sauce can likewise be tailored to personal taste: Walnuts can substitute for pine nuts, and parsley or cilantro can be used instead of basil.

4 SERVINGS

1 tablespoon pine nuts
2 tablespoons extra-virgin olive oil
4 large shallots, cut into thin rings
½ cup dry white wine
2 tablespoons champagne vinegar
1 teaspoon Roasted Garlic Purée
    (see Index)
1 teaspoon coarsely chopped basil
1 teaspoon freshly grated Parmesan cheese
4 (3-ounce) pieces firm white fish fillet
    (such as grouper or red snapper),
    with skin
4 (3-ounce) pieces salmon fillet, with skin
4 (3-ounce) pieces tuna fillet, with skin
Salt and freshly ground black pepper
Clove-Boiled Potatoes (recipe follows)

Preheat the oven to 400 degrees F.

Spread the pine nuts in a single layer in a pie pan. Roast in the hot oven until golden brown, about 5 minutes, shaking the pan after 2 or 3 minutes. Remove from the oven and cool completely.

In a small saucepan, heat 1 tablespoon of the oil over moderately high heat until it begins to sizzle. Add the shallots and sauté for 1 minute, then add the wine, vinegar, garlic purée, basil, and pine nuts. Reduce the heat to low and simmer for 1 minute, then stir in the Parmesan. Remove from the direct heat and keep warm over simmering water.

Place the remaining tablespoon oil in a large bowl. Add the fish to the bowl and toss in the oil until coated. Season the mixture with salt and pepper.

Preheat a griddle or large skillet. Sear the pieces of fish, skin side down, on the hot griddle for 1 minute. Turn and sear the other side for 1 minute. Remove from the griddle and arrange the fish on a platter. Cover with the pesto sauce and serve with Clove-Boiled Potatoes on the side.

❦

CLOVE-BOILED POTATOES

2 pounds red bliss or new potatoes
1 bay leaf
10 whole black peppercorns
3 whole cloves
Pinch of salt

Place the ingredients in a large saucepan and add water just to cover. Place a lid on the pan and cook the potatoes at a low boil until tender, 15 to 17 minutes. Drain, discard the cloves, peppercorns, and bay leaf, and serve immediately.

From *the commonplace to the sublime—the fricassee soars to new heights with a fresh seafood filling and sophisticated presentation.*

Preheat the oven to 375 degrees F.

Layer the five sheets of phyllo on a flat surface and cut into 3-inch-wide strips. On a baking sheet, set two #10 cans (6 inches in diameter) on their sides and drape each with two strips of phyllo. Brush the dough with olive oil and bake in the hot oven until golden brown, 15 to 20 minutes.

Remove the cans from the oven and let cool, then gently pry the phyllo from the cans. Place each phyllo "collar" on a serving plate and set aside.

In a large heavy skillet, heat the canola oil over moderately high heat until almost smoking. Season the snapper fillets on both sides with salt and pepper, then place in the skillet and sauté for 1 minute per side in the hot oil. Remove from the pan and keep warm.

To the skillet, add the lobster, shrimp, and squid. Cook over high heat, stirring, for about a minute, then remove the seafood from the pan and set aside.

To the skillet, add the mussels, shallots, garlic, fennel, bay leaf, and clove. Sauté for about 2 minutes, until the mussels begin to open, then stir in the red wine and fish stock. With a slotted spoon, remove the mussels from the pan and set aside.

Lower the heat to medium and reduce the liquid in the pan by half. In a small bowl, mix the arrowroot with 2 tablespoons of stock from the skillet. Blend until smooth, then stir into the reduced liquid. Fold in the oysters and simmer for 1 minute.

Return the lobster, shrimp, squid, and mussels to the pan. Simmer for 1 minute, then remove the mixture from the heat. Discard the clove.

While hot, spoon the seafood and sauce into the rounded part of the phyllo collars. Arrange a snapper fillet on top and garnish with fronds of fennel. Serve immediately.

4 SERVINGS

5 (12-by-12-inch) sheets phyllo dough
Extra-virgin olive oil, for brushing on the
    phyllo dough
¼ cup canola oil
4 red snapper fillets, with skin, about
    2 ounces each
1 raw lobster tail, from a 1½ pound lobster,
    shelled and cut into 8 medallions
4 large shrimp, peeled and deveined
2 squid, cleaned and sliced into thin rings
8 mussels, scrubbed and debearded
2 shallots, finely chopped
1 clove garlic
1 tablespoon finely shredded fennel bulb
1 bay leaf
1 whole clove
½ cup full-bodied red wine
½ cup Fish Stock (see Index)
1 tablespoon arrowroot
4 shucked oysters
Salt and freshly ground black pepper
8 fennel fronds (sprigs), for garnish

This appetizer or light entrée is derived from an Indian snack called onion bhajia, which is similar to Japanese tempura.

4 SERVINGS

1 large Vidalia onion (any mild, sweet
   onion may be substituted)
1 tablespoon all-purpose flour
1 ½ teaspoons curry powder
2 ounces sole fillet, finely julienned
2 ounces peeled and deveined shrimp,
   finely julienned
2 ounces cleaned squid, finely julienned
1 teaspoon egg white
2 tablespoons Red Pepper Oil (see Index)
Salt and freshly ground black pepper
Chilled mango or papaya, for serving
Lime wedges, yellow bell pepper strips,
   and fresh thyme, for garnish (optional)

Preheat the oven to 450 degrees F.

With a mandoline, food processor, or a very sharp knife, slice the onion as thinly as possible across the diameter. Separate the slices into rings and spread the rings on a dry kitchen towel. Cover with another towel and let dry for 1 hour.

In a shallow bowl, combine the flour, curry powder, and a pinch each of salt and pepper.

Place the shredded seafood in a medium bowl. Add the onion and egg white to the seafood and mix thoroughly. Toss the seafood mixture in the curried flour and shake to remove any excess flour. Divide the seafood mixture into four equal parts and form by hand into loose balls.

In a heavy ovenproof skillet, heat the red pepper oil over moderately high heat until almost smoking. Cook the onion balls in the hot oil until crisp on the bottom, about 2 minutes, then transfer the skillet to the hot oven. Roast until the onion balls are crisp, about 15 minutes.

Remove from the oven and drain on paper towels.

Serve warm onion balls with slices of chilled mango or papaya. Garnish with lime wedges, yellow bell pepper strips, and thyme.

Most fish terrines are assembled and cooked from the outside in by an external heat source. In this recipe, the fish goes directly from the grill into molds, then into the refrigerator, thus maximizing flavor and minimizing vitamin loss.

Preheat a grill. In a medium sauté pan, heat 2 tablespoons oil over moderately high heat until nearly smoking. Add the mushrooms to the hot oil and sauté until soft, about 3 minutes. Remove the mushrooms from the heat, drain, and set aside.

Lay the halibut and salmon on a flat surface and, holding the knife parallel to the work surface, slice each fillet horizontally into three thin pieces. Season the slices on both sides with herbes de Provence, salt, and pepper. Brush each slice with oil and place on the hot grill. Sear for about 2 minutes per side, until the flesh loses its translucency. Remove from the grill and keep warm.

Line a 9-by-5-by-2¾-inch terrine or loaf pan with a sheet of plastic wrap large enough to overlap the long sides by 4 inches. Fill terrine, beginning with a slice of salmon. Cover salmon with a layer of mushrooms, followed by a slice of halibut and a layer of tomatoes. Continue to layer terrine, alternating the ingredients. When the terrine is nearly full, fold the plastic wrap over the top and set another pan, the same size, inside of it. Fill the top pan with water so that the terrine is compressed, and refrigerate for 48 hours.

Just before serving, remove the top pan and invert the terrine onto a platter. Serve slices of the terrine accompanied by Orange and Pernod Salad.

❦

Combine all the ingredients, except the lettuce, in a medium bowl and toss. Divide the lettuce leaves among four plates and spoon the orange mixture on top.

4 SERVINGS

2 tablespoons extra-virgin olive oil, plus more for brushing on the fish
8 ounces cremini mushrooms, stems removed
1 halibut fillet, about 1 pound
1 salmon fillet, about 1 pound
Pinch of herbes de Provence
4 ripe tomatoes, peeled, seeded, and sliced
Salt and freshly ground black pepper
Orange and Pernod Salad (recipe follows)

ORANGE AND PERNOD SALAD

4 oranges, peeled and segmented
6 fresh mint leaves, finely shredded
2 tablespoons Pernod
Scant pinch of crushed red pepper
Pinch of freshly ground black pepper
4 large lettuce leaves

After years of making the classic bouillabaisse from Provence, I decided to adapt the recipe using seafood native to southeastern Louisiana. When making this dish at home, use fish and shellfish indigenous to your area, if possible. I think you'll be pleasantly surprised at the flavor provided by virtually any combination of shellfish—for example, lobsters, crabs, and mussels—and firm-fleshed fish, such as snapper or grouper.

4 TO 6 SERVINGS

¼ cup extra-virgin olive oil
4 red drum fillets, about 2 ounces each
8 ounces medium shrimp, peeled and deveined
4 grouper fillets, about 2 ounces each
1 onion, finely chopped
1 leek, white part only, finely chopped
2 cloves garlic, crushed
Pinch of saffron threads
1 tablespoon chopped fresh parsley
1 small bay leaf
¼ teaspoon fresh savory leaves
¼ teaspoon fennel seeds
1 tomato, peeled, seeded, and chopped
8 new potatoes, peeled and halved
1 carrot, finely shredded
6 cups Infused Fish Stock (recipe follows)
4 ounces lump crab meat, picked over to remove any shell and cartilage
4 ounces peeled crawfish
8 oysters, shucked
Salt and freshly ground black pepper
Fresh Croutons (see Index)

Heat the oil in a large pot over moderately high heat until it is very hot and starts to smoke. Add the red drum and sear on both sides, about 30 seconds per side. Remove from the pan and drain on paper towels. Add the shrimp to the pan and sear, tossing frequently, about 1 minute. Remove the shrimp from the pan with a slotted spoon. Repeat with the grouper, searing it for about 30 seconds on each side. Set the red drum, shrimp, and grouper aside.

To the hot oil, add the onion, leek, garlic, saffron, parsley, bay leaf, savory, and fennel seeds. Sauté until the onion is clear and tender, then add the tomato. When the tomato softens and breaks apart, add the potatoes, carrot, and Infused Fish Stock. Bring the mixture to a boil, then reduce the heat and simmer for 15 minutes.

Return the red drum, shrimp, and grouper to the pot and simmer for a couple of minutes; do not overcook. Remove the pot from the heat and fold in the crab meat and crawfish. Adjust the seasoning with salt and pepper.

Just before serving, place one or two oysters in the center of each bowl and spoon fish, shrimp, and stock over the oysters. Serve with Fresh Croutons.

❦

INFUSED FISH STOCK

1 tablespoon extra-virgin olive oil
½ fennel bulb, finely shredded
1 tablespoon tomato paste
2 oranges, cut into quarters
1 lemon, halved
6 cups Fish Stock (see Index)

In a large saucepan, heat the oil over moderately high heat until it begins to sizzle. Add the fennel and sauté until soft, about 5 minutes. Stir in the tomato paste and cook for 2 minutes, then add the oranges, lemon, and fish stock. Reduce the heat and simmer for 15 minutes. Strain and cool to room temperature. Use immediately or cover and refrigerate for up to 2 days.

*P*rior to adding the scallops to this soup, I grill them lightly to imbue them with a hint of the appealing flavor of the grill. The resulting smokiness melds with the other ingredients in this recipe to produce a complex-flavored soup that is just as good served cold as warm.

Heat charcoal in a barbecue grill until ashen. Brush the grill rack with oil and place the scallops on the hot grill; sear on the top and bottom, about 30 seconds per side. Slice each scallop in half across the diameter and return to the grill. Score on the two remaining unscored sides, remove from the heat, and set aside.

Split the cucumbers lengthwise, remove any seeds, and slice crosswise as thinly as possible. Place the slices in a colander positioned over a bowl and sprinkle with the salt. Toss to coat the slices, then let sit for 20 minutes. Rinse thoroughly with cold running water. Drain, then dry the slices on paper towels.

In a large saucepan, heat the remaining tablespoon of oil until almost smoking. Add the shallots and garlic, and sauté until tender and glossy. Add the cucumber and bay leaf; cook for 5 minutes, then stir in the stock and vermouth. Bring the mixture to a slow boil and simmer for 3 minutes. Add the grilled scallops and simmer until heated through, about 2 minutes.

Remove the scallops with a slotted spoon and divide among the soup bowls. Remove and discard the bay leaf. Adjust the seasoning with pepper, then add the cream, dill, and tomato.

Remove the soup from the heat, spoon it around the scallops, and serve immediately. Alternatively, this soup can be served chilled.

4 TO 6 SERVINGS

1 tablespoon extra-virgin olive oil, plus
    more for brushing on the grill rack
12 large sea scallops
2 European cucumbers, peeled
1 tablespoon salt
4 shallots, finely chopped
1 clove garlic, finely chopped
1 bay leaf
2 cups Chicken Stock (see Index)
1 cup dry vermouth
2 tablespoons heavy cream
1 teaspoon finely chopped fresh dill
1 very ripe tomato, peeled, seeded, and
    finely diced
Freshly ground black pepper

In my mind, one of the most important culinary legacies of the American Indian is corn and shellfish soup. Today, any coastal town in any region of North America serves its own delicious version. Fortunately, this soup can be prepared with flash-frozen corn kernels, since good fresh corn is sometimes unavailable.

4 SERVINGS

4 ears sweet corn, shucked, or 2 cups
    frozen corn kernels
2 tablespoons unsalted butter
1 medium onion, chopped
1 bay leaf
Pinch of fresh thyme
1 small jalapeño pepper, seeded and
    finely diced
1 medium Idaho potato, peeled and
    finely sliced
4 cups Chicken Stock (see Index)
1 pound lump crab meat, picked over to
    remove any shell and cartilage
Salt and freshly ground black pepper
Warm bread or Garlic Melba Toast
    (see Index)
Scallion rings and fresh parsley, for
    garnish (optional)

In a large pot, bring 8 cups salted water to a boil. Immerse the corn in the water and boil for 1 minute, then plunge the ears into ice water. Drain and scrape the kernels from the cobs with a sharp knife.

In another large pot, melt the butter over medium heat. Add the onion, bay leaf, thyme, and jalapeño, and cook until the onion is clear and tender. Add the potato, corn kernels, and chicken stock, and simmer for 15 to 20 minutes, until the potato begins to fall apart when pierced with a fork.

Remove the bay leaf and purée the soup in a food processor or blender for 4 to 5 minutes, until smooth; process in batches if necessary. Adjust the seasoning with salt and pepper, then pour into a clean saucepan. Fold in the crab meat and warm over low heat. Serve with slices of warm bread or Garlic Melba Toast. Garnish with scallion rings and parsley, if desired.

I'm always looking for ways to reduce fat while maintaining flavor. In this appetizer or light main course, tender artichoke leaves stand in for the traditional calorie-laden pizza crust.

Preheat the oven to 375 degrees F.

Cook the artichokes according to the instructions on page 94. Pull the tender outer leaves from the artichokes and pare the hearts.

On four large ovenproof dinner plates, arrange a single layer of artichoke leaves, leaf tips pointing out; leave a 3-inch round space in the center of the plate. In the same manner, form a smaller ring of artichoke leaves on top of the bottom layer, so that the plate resembles a flower. Cut the artichoke hearts into thin slices and mound an equal amount in the center of each plate.

In a medium bowl, combine the shrimp, scallops, mussels, and squid. In another bowl, combine the ricotta, chèvre, and Parmesan. Set both mixtures aside.

Spoon Tomato Concasse on top of the sliced artichoke hearts. Dot the artichoke leaves with the seafood and cheese mixtures. Drizzle olive oil over the pizza and, if desired, garnish with black olives.

Place the pizzas in the hot oven and cook until the cheese melts, about 5 minutes. Serve hot.

4 SERVINGS

4 medium artichokes
8 ounces cooked baby shrimp
8 ounces bay scallops
8 ounces cooked mussels
8 ounces cooked squid, cut into rings
½ cup ricotta cheese
4 ounces soft, mild chèvre cheese
¼ cup freshly grated Parmesan cheese
1 cup Tomato Concasse (see Index)
¼ cup extra-virgin olive oil
¼ cup sliced pitted black olives (optional)

Instead of pork or beef casings, I use plastic wrap to encase my seafood sausage. You can use prefabricated synthetic casings if you prefer, but check the contents carefully, since these are often meat-protein based.

4 SERVINGS

1 tablespoon extra-virgin olive oil
1 clove garlic, finely chopped
2 shallots, finely diced
Pinch of herbes de Provence
Pinch of five-spice powder (available
    at specialty food stores and
    Asian markets)
8 ounces grouper fillet, cut into
    ½-inch dice
8 ounces salmon fillet, cut into
    ½-inch dice
8 ounces peeled shrimp, cut into
    ½-inch dice
8 ounces shelled lobster, cut into ½-inch
    dice (reserve the tomalley; see Note)
Salt and freshly ground black pepper
Warm Mustard Sauce (recipe follows)

In a small skillet, heat the oil over moderately high heat until it releases its aroma. Add the garlic and shallots, and sauté in the hot oil for 2 to 3 minutes, until the shallots are tender. Stir in the herbes de Provence and five-spice powder. Remove the mixture from the heat and let cool.

Place the grouper, salmon, shrimp, and lobster in a large bowl. Add the cooled garlic and shallots. Season with salt and pepper and blend thoroughly. Fold in the tomalley, if there is any. Cover with plastic wrap and refrigerate for 2 hours.

Spoon the chilled sausage filling into a pastry bag fitted with a 1-inch plain tube. Spread a sheet of plastic wrap, about 6 by 12 inches, on a flat surface. On the long end of the sheet, pipe a line of filling from one edge to the other. Roll the filling in the wrap and fold the ends several times to seal the sausage. Repeat the process with the remaining filling, making 3 to 4 sausages in all.

Cook the sausages either by steaming, poaching, or roasting. To steam, place over simmering water in a covered bamboo steamer for 20 minutes. To poach, simmer in 1 gallon court-bouillon (for recipe, see page 147) for 5 minutes. To roast, spread on a baking sheet and place in a 375 degree F. oven for 7 to 10 minutes.

Let the sausages rest for 2 to 3 minutes after cooking, then unwrap and cut each sausage on the diagonal into ½-inch slices. Fan the slices on four serving plates and place a small bowl of Warm Mustard Sauce in the center of each plate for dipping.

Note: Tomalley, the moss green liver of the lobster, is small enough to fit into a tablespoon. Like roe, it is considered a delicacy and should be frozen and reserved for flavoring other dishes.

❦

Combine the mustard, honey, and yogurt in a small bowl. Blend to a smooth paste. Add the hoisin sauce, soy sauce, ginger, and scallions. If the mixture appears too thick, dilute with a little warm water. Serve at room temperature.

WARM MUSTARD SAUCE

2 teaspoons dry mustard
¼ cup lukewarm honey
2 tablespoons lukewarm plain yogurt
1 teaspoon hoisin sauce
1 teaspoon soy sauce
½ teaspoon grated fresh ginger
2 scallions, finely sliced

❧ *Stocks, Seasonings, & Seafood Combinations* ❧

Finnan haddie takes its name from Findon, Scotland, reputedly the source of the finest smoked haddock available. Typically smoked haddock is baked, broiled, or poached, but here it graces a fish soup.

6 SERVINGS

4 smoked haddock fillets, about 3 to 4
   ounces each
1 tablespoon light vegetable oil
1 white onion, finely diced
1 bay leaf
2 Idaho potatoes, peeled and finely diced
3 cups Fish Stock (see Index)
Tomato Concasse (recipe follows)
4 teaspoons heavy cream
2 tablespoons finely chopped fresh chives
Freshly ground black pepper

Prior to cooking, soak the haddock in cold water for 1 hour, changing the water several times during the hour. Soaking will flush out excess salt and plump the fillets.

In a large sauté pan, heat the oil over moderately high heat until almost smoking. Add the onion and cook until glossy, then stir in the bay leaf and potatoes. Sauté for 5 minutes, then add the fish stock. Bring the mixture to a low boil, then place the fillets in the pan and cook for 3 minutes.

Remove the haddock from the pan and let cool. Peel off the skin and remove all the bones. Gently flake the flesh into a bowl and set aside.

Continue to simmer the potatoes in the stock until the pieces fall apart when pierced with a fork. Discard bay leaf. Transfer the mixture to a blender or food processor and blend until smooth. Pour the purée into a saucepan and keep warm. Season with pepper to taste. Fold in the flaked haddock and simmer until warmed through.

Ladle into warmed soup bowls and garnish with a spoonful of Tomato Concasse. Before serving, drizzle a teaspoon of cream into each bowl of soup and sprinkle with chopped chives.

❤

TOMATO CONCASSE

1 tablespoon extra-virgin olive oil
4 shallots, finely chopped
2 cloves garlic, finely chopped
1 bay leaf
1 sprig fresh thyme
Pinch of fresh rosemary
6 very ripe tomatoes, peeled, seeded,
   and diced
½ cup dry vermouth
Salt and freshly ground black pepper

In a heavy skillet, heat the oil over moderately high heat until almost smoking. Add the shallots, garlic, bay leaf, thyme, and rosemary. Cook over moderate heat until the shallots are tender, about 3 minutes, then add the tomatoes. Bring the mixture to a boil, then cook over medium heat for 10 minutes, stirring frequently. Add the vermouth and simmer until reduced by half, another 10 minutes. Adjust the seasoning with salt and pepper, remove from the heat, and let cool to room temperature. Discard bay leaf.

Crab meat, cheese, sausage, and other traditional fillings for mushrooms are so pungent that they overshadow their mushroom host. Here, the non-traditional cold horseradish and roe filling shares center stage with the warm creminis.

4 SERVINGS

2 tablespoons finely chopped onion
16 large cremini mushrooms
Extra-virgin olive oil, for brushing on
    mushrooms
1 teaspoon finely grated fresh horseradish
2 ounces (¼ cup) salmon caviar, chilled
½ teaspoon chopped fresh chervil
Salt and freshly ground black pepper

Place the onion in a strainer and rinse under cold running water. Drain thoroughly.

Preheat the broiler. Remove the stems from the mushrooms and trim the gills, or indentations, in the caps to form tiny cups. Brush the mushrooms with oil and season with salt and pepper. Place on a baking sheet and broil until tender, about 5 minutes.

While the mushrooms are cooking, combine the onion and horseradish in a small bowl. Remove the mushrooms from the broiler and divide among four serving plates. Place about ¼ teaspoon of the horseradish mixture in each mushroom. Top with the salmon caviar and sprinkle with the chervil. Serve immediately.

❦ ROASTED GARLIC PURÉE ❦

Roasted garlic has a sweet, mellow flavor and a buttery texture.

MAKES ABOUT 2 TABLESPOONS

1 large head garlic
Extra-virgin olive oil, for brushing

Preheat the oven to 400 degrees F.

Brush or rub the garlic with oil and wrap in aluminum foil. Seal tightly and place in the hot oven for 15 minutes.

Remove from the oven and let cool. Unwrap the garlic and squeeze out the pulp.

*T*he *traditional pot-au-feu features beef and chicken accompanied by vege-*
tables. The ingredients and quick method of cooking lend this more contem-
porary version an Oriental cast.

Star anise is an Asian spice that can be purchased either whole or ground.
Always use this licorice-flavored seasoning judiciously, as it is most potent.

Roast the red pepper under the broiler as close to the heat as possible, turning frequently, until blistered and charred all over. Remove from the heat and scrape off the blackened skin. Shred the flesh and set aside.

Cook the noodles in boiling salted water for 2 to 3 minutes, until tender. Rinse and drain in a colander.

In a large skillet or wok, heat the oil over moderately high heat until almost smoking. When the oil is hot, add the lobster, shrimp, scallops, and mussels. Sauté until the mussels open, then remove the shellfish from the pan and keep warm.

To the pan, add the leek, star anise, garlic, lemon juice, and bay leaf. Cook over high heat for about a minute, stirring, then add the fish stock. Bring to a boil and reduce for 4 minutes over high heat. Stir in the snow peas and roasted bell pepper. Return the shellfish to the pan. Bring the mixture back to a boil and add the noodles. Discard the star anise and bay leaf. Sprinkle with the cilantro leaves and serve.

4 SERVINGS

½ red bell pepper
1 (8-ounce) package Japanese soba noodles (buckwheat noodles available in Asian markets)
2 tablespoons light vegetable oil
2 raw lobster tails in the shell, cut into 8 pieces
6 large shrimp, peeled and deveined
6 sea scallops
16 mussels in their shells, debearded
1 leek, white part only, finely shredded
2 whole star anise
1 clove garlic, crushed
Juice of 1 lemon
1 bay leaf
4 cups Fish Stock (see Index)
10 snow peas, finely shredded
20 fresh cilantro leaves

❦ FISH STOCK ❦

This stock calls for the bones of any cold-water fish because cold-water species are far less oily than their warm-water counterparts, and, therefore, their bones do not cloud the stock. The taste and color of the basic recipe can be modified with the addition of other ingredients; tomato skins or saffron will turn the stock a rich gold, while citrus fruit or fresh herbs, like tarragon or mint, will alter the flavor of the infusion.

MAKES ABOUT 4 QUARTS

¼ cup light vegetable oil
4 pounds cold-water fish bones (such as
    sole, turbot, halibut, or whiting),
    thoroughly washed and cut to a
    manageable size
2 medium onions, finely diced
1 small bunch celery, finely diced
1 bunch parsley, chopped
2 leeks, white part only, chopped
2 bay leaves
1 sprig fresh thyme
2 cups dry white wine

In a large stockpot, heat the oil over moderately high heat until almost smoking. Add the fish bones, onions, celery, parsley, leeks, bay leaves, and thyme, raise the heat to high, and sauté, stirring constantly, until the onions become translucent. Remove the pot from the heat, cover, and let sit for 10 minutes.

Return the pot to high heat and add the wine and 1 gallon cold water. Bring to a boil, uncovered, skimming any foam from the surface. Reduce the heat to medium and cook for 30 minutes.

Remove the stock from the heat and skim the surface a final time. Strain and cool to room temperature. Store in the refrigerator for up to 5 days or freeze indefinitely.

❦ CHICKEN STOCK ❦

Rather than rely on the canned variety, it is well worth the effort to make a homemade chicken stock.

MAKES ABOUT 3 QUARTS

4 pounds chicken bones
2 onions, chopped
4 ribs celery, chopped
2 leeks, white part only, chopped
1 bay leaf
10 white peppercorns
1 sprig fresh thyme
1 clove garlic

Combine all the ingredients in a heavy stockpot. Add 1 gallon cold water. Bring the mixture to a boil over high heat, skimming any scum that forms on the surface. Lower the heat and simmer, uncovered, for 1 hour; skim occasionally.

Remove the stock from the heat and skim the surface a final time. Strain and cool to room temperature. Store in the refrigerator for up to 1 week or freeze indefinitely.

The scraps from any crustaceans, including shrimp and crawfish, can be used instead of lobster to flavor this stock.

In a heavy stockpot, heat the oil over moderately high heat until almost smoking. Add the chopped lobster and cook until pink, about 4 minutes. Add the garlic, onion, carrot, celery, bay leaves, tarragon, and peppercorns. When the onion becomes glossy, add the cayenne pepper, tomatoes, white wine, Madeira, and brandy, along with 1 gallon water.

Bring the mixture to a rolling boil, then reduce the heat and simmer, uncovered, for 45 minutes. Strain, let cool, and refrigerate for up to several days. The stock will freeze indefinitely in sealed containers.

MAKES ABOUT 3 QUARTS

¼ cup light vegetable oil
6 lobster carcasses, chopped (or 2 whole
    lobsters, about 1¼ pounds each,
    chopped)
2 cloves garlic, finely chopped
1 large white onion, chopped
1 carrot, chopped
4 ribs celery, chopped
2 bay leaves
1 tablespoon fresh tarragon leaves
1 teaspoon black peppercorns
Pinch of cayenne pepper
6 very ripe tomatoes, roughly chopped
1 cup dry white wine
1 cup Madeira
1 cup brandy

❦ BODY CONSCIOUS PEPPER ❦

This all-purpose mixture will keep indefinitely in the refrigerator and can be used to season any type of fish or seafood.

Combine all the ingredients in a blender and process for about a minute, just until the mixture forms a coarse powder. Transfer to an airtight container until ready to use.

MAKES ABOUT 1½ CUPS

3 tablespoons freshly ground white pepper
3 tablespoons freshly ground black pepper
2 tablespoons mustard seeds
2 tablespoons fennel seeds
2 tablespoons celery seeds
2 tablespoons finely chopped storebought
    or homemade dried lemon peel;
    see instructions on page 30
2 tablespoons finely chopped storebought
    or homemade dried orange peel;
    see instructions for drying lemon peel
    on page 30
3 tablespoons whole pink peppercorns,
    crushed

This glossary deals only with the fish and shellfish called for in the recipes in this book. It can be used as a specific reference tool as well as for general background information.

ABALONE

Abalone is a gastropod, which means that it is a mollusk with a single shell and a single muscle. In appearance, it can be compared to a large, single-shelled clam or a human ear (its generic name, *Haliotis*, is derived from two Greek words meaning "sea ear"). It is found clinging to rocks (its shell-less side closest to the rocks) off the coasts of California, Alaska, Chile, and Southeast Asia, and is farmed elsewhere, including California and Hawaii. The largest of the many species of abalone is the red abalone, which can reach 8 pounds in weight and 12 inches in length, making it about twice as large as the average abalone.

The availability of abalone is limited and when it is for sale it tends to be expensive. When prepared well, that is to say tenderized and not overcooked—no more than 45 seconds per side—its flavor is mild and sweet and its texture is firm but meltingly smooth. The iridescent interior of the abalone shell is the ever-popular mother-of-pearl; the outside of the shell can be pink, red, green, or black.

Abalone is commonly eaten lightly fried or raw. If fresh abalone isn't available, conch or geoduck, a large soft-shell clam from the Pacific Northwest, can often be substituted. Abalone is available canned, dried, or salted as well as fresh.

AMBERJACK

Amberjack is a member of the jack family, which includes about 140 species, including Florida pompano and the yellowtail of Japan. There are several species of amberjack, but the most significant is greater amberjack, which lives in tropical and warm waters and migrates into higher latitudes during the summer months. This fish can weigh up to 175 pounds but it is the much smaller amberjacks—those weighing about 15 pounds—that are considered best for eating. The flesh is meaty and rich.

When buying large amberjacks from the southeastern United States it is important to watch for parasitic worms embedded in the muscle. Though aesthetically displeasing, these are easy to remove, and cooking or adequate freezing destroys them. Large amberjack caught around tropical islands should not be eaten at all because they may cause ciguatera poisoning, a debilitating but generally not fatal illness caused by a toxin that is produced by a tropical marine algae and works its way up the food chain, accumulating in large predatory fish like amberjack.

Amberjack is an ideal fish for chowder. If amberjack is unavailable, yellowtail and mahi mahi (also known as dolphin fish) are acceptable substitutes.

BRILL

Brill is a flatfish that is found only in European waters around the Mediterranean and the Eastern Atlantic north to Norway. It is similar to turbot but is smaller—it can weigh as much as 15 pounds but is more commonly 2 to 4 pounds—is more oval in shape, and has smooth as opposed to bumpy skin. Like turbot, both of its eyes are on the left side of its body. Its flesh is delicate and light.

A small quantity of brill is imported into the United States but it tends to be expensive and hard to find. Sand dab (called windowpane, daylight, and sundial by recreational fishermen who often throw it back) is a suitable substitute, although it is somewhat difficult to fillet. Other possible substitutes include East Coast fluke, Gulf of Mexico southern flounder, and petrale sole.

CARP

Carp has a long history, having been pond-cultured by the Chinese since 500 B.C. and written about by Aristotle around 350 B.C. Carp is a hardy fish, able to withstand varying conditions, including water temperatures as high as 96°F for up to 24 hours as well as temporary freezing. The best carp for eating comes from cold, flowing waters as the organic matter that carp consume in warm water give this fish a mossy flavor. The white meat of the carp is firm-textured and sweet whereas the dark meat is tough and not usually recommended for consumption. Carp is the most common base for gefilte fish, which is traditionally served during the Jewish Passover Seder. Carp roe is sometimes used as a substitute for caviar.

If carp is unavailable, buffalofish can be substituted in many recipes.

CATFISH

Catfish have long, fluid bodies and "whiskers" (actually barbels) on their lips that are used to locate food. The flesh is firm and sweet-textured. In the past some people complained that catfish flesh tasted muddy—wild catfish feed from the bottom of rivers—but this is no longer a serious problem because most catfish are now farm-raised in large ponds under controlled conditions. The annual harvest is over 150,000 tons, making catfish farming the largest fish-farming industry in the United States. Most of the catfish in this country come from Mississippi, but Arkansas, Alabama, Louisiana, Georgia, Idaho, California, North Carolina, and South Carolina are big producers as well. Whereas farmed catfish usually weigh between 2 and 3 pounds, wild catfish can range in weight from 8 ounces to over 50 pounds. Wild and imported catfish tend to be less expensive than domestic farm-raised catfish, but because they are not subjected to the same rigorous quality testing, they are not always of comparable eating quality.

Whitefish, sole, and perch are acceptable substitutes for catfish in many recipes.

CAVIAR

Genuine caviar, perhaps the most luxurious of all foods, is the cleaned, lightly salted roe, or eggs, of female sturgeon, most of which come from the Caspian and Black seas. The largest eggs come from the largest sturgeon (which can reach 12 feet in length, carry 45 pounds or more of eggs, and live to the ripe old age of one hundred years) and are processed to make the most expensive and popular of caviars, known as beluga. Also enjoyed by connoisseurs are osetra caviar and sevruga caviar (the most widely available variety), the eggs for which come from successively smaller sturgeon. Pressed caviar is made from the smaller damaged and less firm eggs that are sifted out when the other types of caviar are being processed.

The eggs for caviar are collected during the spawning season when the fish swim from the deep ocean waters to shallow riverbeds, where they are caught and transferred to submerged floating cages. The fish, unable to find food in the cages, are forced to live off the fat in the roe, thus removing excess oil from it. When the roe is ready for salting, it is removed from the live fish, which are then set free.

In addition to "genuine" caviar, numerous other caviars are made from the eggs of different kinds of fish—for example, salmon, lumpfish, herring, mullet, and shad. They are all less expensive than sturgeon caviar.

Good caviar is whole, crisp, and firm. It should "pop" when eaten. There are those who believe that caviar is an aphrodisiac, although there is no scientific evidence to prove it.

CHAR

Char are members of the trout and salmon family Salmonidae. When used in North America, the term "char" refers to the Arctic char (there are both sea-run and landlocked populations), a fish that is a staple among Eskimos and is well known in Northern European markets, in the Alpine regions of Western Europe, as well as in England; for centuries the English have used a very small char to make char pie or potted char. Generally sea-run char are considered better than the landlocked char, boasting very firm, rich flesh with a small flake.

If char is unavailable, trout or salmon can be substituted in many recipes.

CLAMS

Clams, bivalve (double-shelled) mollusks that live buried in sand or mud, usually in inshore waters, throughout much of the world, can be divided into two distinct categories: those with hard shells and those with soft (thin and fragile) shells.

Hard-Shell Clams

Hard-shell clams are also known, at least on the East Coast, by their Algonquin Indian name, quahogs, pronounced ko-hogs. (The shells, which have easily visible growth bands, were used as currency among Native Americans until the end of the seventeenth century.) The East Coast varieties of hard-shell clams can be broken down into three main categories: littlenecks, cherrystones, and chowder clams. Littlenecks are the smallest and most expensive of the bunch and are commonly served raw, on the half shell. Cherrystones, the next size up, can also be served on the half shell but are more often used in chowders and baked dishes (they are the shining stars of the famous New England clambake). Chowder clams are older, tougher, and larger than littlenecks and cherrystones and are most often chopped or minced.

The best known of the Pacific Coast varieties of hard-shell clams are Pacific littlenecks and Manilas, which were accidental imports in the 1930s, tagging along when the Japanese oyster seed was introduced to Washington State bays. Both Pacific littlenecks (also known as rock clams) and Manilas are commonly served steamed; Manilas are also served raw.

Soft-Shell Clams

Soft-shell clams, also called soft clams, have thin shells that do not close completely because of a rubbery black or brown neck (or siphon) that extends beyond the edges of the shells. The most well known of the East Coast varieties is the steamer clam (also known as the longneck, belly clam, and Ipswitch), and it is often served fried, steamed, or raw.

Of the West Coast varieties of soft-shell clams the best known are razor clams and geoducks. Razor clams owe their name to their sharp, brittle shells (which have been compared to old-fashioned straight-edged razors) and are commonly minced for fritters or steamed. There is an East Coast razor clam but it is rarely harvested. Geoducks (pronounced gooey-ducks) are found only in the Pacific Northwest and are the giants of the North American clam world: They can reach 5 pounds in weight (3 pounds is more typical), and their necks can exceed 3 feet in length. Geoduck meat, often fried or grilled as steaks (about three per clam), is reminiscent of abalone. The neck is rubbery and tough but can be skinned, cut into thin strips, and tenderized with a mallet, or minced for chowders or dips.

COD

Fishermen from Europe were landing cod from the North Atlantic long before the first settlements were established in North America, and there are historians who hypothesize that the superabundance of cod in the North Atlantic was one of the factors that prompted colonization. Cape Cod was named after this cold-water fish, and since 1784 a large white pine carving of the "Sacred Cod" has hung in the Massachusetts State House in Boston, a city that garnered much of its wealth from the cod trade.

Among the best known members of the cod family are haddock and pollock, both of which have firm, white, lean flesh. Scrod (sometimes spelled and pronounced "shrod") is not the name of a species of fish, but the term for small (1½ to 2½ pounds) cod, haddock, pollock, or cusk, a cousin of cod.

CONCH

When Christopher Columbus landed in the Bahamas in 1492, he noted that the Arawak Indians made full use of the conch (pronounced konk), eating the meat and using the spiral-shaped shells to make chisels, cutting tools, trumpets, and ceremonial carvings.

Like abalone, the conch is a gastropod mollusk (a mollusk with a single shell and a single muscle) that yields tough meat that must be tenderized. It is found in southern waters and is most popular in the Caribbean and the Florida Keys; in fact, "Conch" is a nickname for a native or resident of the Florida Keys. Conch is sometimes confused with whelk, which, while related, belongs to a different part of the mollusk family. Conch meat has a mild clamlike flavor. If conch is unavailable, abalone or whelk are acceptable substitutes.

CRAB

There are more varieties of crabs off the coast of North America than off the coast of any other continent. The most popular species are the King and Dungeness crabs, the stone crab, and the blue crab. The meat of all four kinds is similarly tender, flaky, and delicately sweet.

King crabs are the largest of all crabs. Three species—red, blue, and brown—are found in the North Pacific and the Bering Sea. Red (commercially, the most important) and blue can measure 6 feet across and weigh 20 pounds, though most don't exceed 10 pounds; brown, which inhabit deep waters along the continental shelf, are smaller than the red and blue.

Dungeness crabs are the most commercially important crabs on the West Coast. Named after a small community on the Strait of Juan de Fuca in Washington State, they commonly measure about 6 inches across and weigh in at between 1 and 3 pounds, yielding a higher ratio of meat to shell than most other crabs. The meat is also easier to remove from the shell.

Stone crabs, found in the North Pacific and the Atlantic, are different than the other crabs listed here in that only the claws are used and they are cooked by the fishermen right after capture (because the uncooked meat would stick to the shell if frozen uncooked). Fishermen twist off one claw, then throw the animal back into the water to regenerate another one, which takes about 18 months.

Blue crabs (also known as buffalo crabs) are most abundant in the Chesapeake and Delaware Bay areas but can also be found throughout the Eastern seaboard into the Gulf of Mexico. Their dark bodies, which are accented with bluish tinges, measure between 5 and 7 inches and weigh between 4 and 16 ounces.

Soft-shell crabs are crabs that are caught while "undressed." As crabs mature they periodically outgrow and shed their hard outer shells. If a crab is harvested before it has a chance to replace the old shell with a new slightly larger one, then the crab is deemed "soft-shell" and is almost entirely edible.

CRAWFISH

Crawfish is the Southern name (in addition to crawdads, creekcrabs, yabbies, and mudbugs) for crayfish, the small lobsterlike crustaceans that roam in freshwater throughout much of the world. Most wild as well as farmed crawfish in this country comes from Louisiana (Breaux Bridge was named Crawfish Capital of the World by the Louisiana legislature), where they swim in streams, swamps, bayous, and rice fields, although they are also available commercially from Oregon, California, and Washington. Although over 300 species of crawfish have been named throughout the world, only a few of these species have bodies at least 3½ inches long, considered the minimum size for eating. The meat of the crawfish, most of which is concentrated in the tail, is sweet and tender.

At the end of July and throughout August in much of Scandinavia, especially Finland and Sweden, crawfish are consumed in abundance, accompanied by ice-cold aquavit and mugs of beer. The Louisiana equivalent of the Scandinavian *krebfest* is the famous "Crawfish Boil," a popular event throughout Louisiana during the spring.

EEL

Eels are among the world's most fascinating fish and have long been the source of superstitions and folklore. Some Europeans once thought that rubbing their skin with eel would make them see visions of fairies. There are tribes in the Philippines who believe that eels are the souls of the dead. Like salmon, eels undertake long spawning migrations. American and European eels leave estuaries, tidal marshes, rivers, and lakes in their home waters in order to spawn at great depths in the southwestern part of the Atlantic, known as the Sargasso Sea. Once the spawning is done, they die, probably of fatigue. With the help of the current, however, the eels' transparent leaf-shaped larvae are carried to the continents of Europe and North America, a journey that can take from one to two-and-a-half years or more. As the larvae approach coastal estuaries, they lose their transparency and become miniature eels through metamorphosis, then continue to swim up rivers and streams, crawl up the rocky faces of waterfalls, and slither over damp fields until they find a body of water where they can grow to adulthood. After twelve or more years in freshwater, a biological clock tells these Atlantic-born eels to begin the arduous journey downriver and out to sea to their place of birth in order to spawn and thus complete the cycle of life.

In order to undertake the long spawning migration, the eel must store high levels of unsaturated fat in its muscle, as it does not eat during migration, and it is this fat that makes the snakelike creature so flavorful. Still, flavorful or not, eel has not maintained wide popularity in the United States, even though it was a favorite among the Pilgrims. In Japan and Europe, however, demand exceeds supply. The Japanese have opened restaurants devoted solely to eel, and it is traditionally eaten during the hottest part of the year because the Japanese believe that eating eel helps prevent heat exhaustion. (One of the most popular Japanese eel recipes is charcoal-grilled marinated eel fillet served over rice). In the Netherlands smoked eel is sold in all the market towns during the fall and winter. In The Hague and in Amsterdam sidewalk vendors sell smoked eel sandwiches much like New York City vendors hawk pretzels and hot dogs.

If eel is unavailable, garfish, skate, or catfish can be substituted in many recipes.

FLOUNDER

Flounder is the overall name for three families of flatfish, which together represent over 200 species of fish in the Atlantic and Pacific oceans. Like other flatfish, flounder are flat and oval in shape, have both eyes on one side of their head (the side facing upward), and swim horizontally close to the bottom of the sea.

GARFISH

Garfish is also known as sea-needle (thanks to its pointed beak); green-bone (its backbone really is green); and mackerel scout (because its arrival in coastal waters often precedes that of the mackerel). It is an oceanic fish found from the Mediterranean to the Baltic, Norway, and Iceland. It is a good-tasting fish—one that yields bone-free fillets—that some people misguidedly avoid because of the color of the backbone. Garfish is popular in Scandinavian countries and Denmark in particular.

If garfish is unavailable, fresh sardines can be substituted in many recipes.

GROUPER

This hermaphroditic fish (it begins life as a female, then changes to a male after a few years) is a member of the sea bass family, the largest and most diverse family of fish in the world. The most commonly available groupers in the U.S. market are the red grouper and the black grouper. Not always easy to find but of excellent quality is scamp grouper, one of the smallest groupers roaming the Atlantic. Grouper meat is thick, white, and firm-textured, and has a distinctive yet mild flavor.

If grouper is not available, monkfish, tilefish, snapper, or sea bass are acceptable substitutes in many recipes.

HALIBUT

Pacific, Atlantic, and California are the three types of halibut commonly available in fisheries in the United States.

Pacific halibut (also called northern or Alaska halibut) has firm, mildly flavored flesh and is the most abundant; Atlantic halibut (called chicken halibut when it is under 20 pounds) is mild in flavor and dense; California halibut (also known as bastard and southern halibut) is similar in shape to the Pacific halibut but its meat is coarser and softer in texture.

Like all flounder, halibut begin life with an eye on each side of their heads, but after a few weeks the left eye moves to the right side and the body changes color: The upper (or right) side turns a dark, mottled green-brown to blend in with the bottom of the ocean, and the underside (called the blind side) turns white. Halibut continue to grow throughout their lives and have the potential to reach 9 feet in length and 600 pounds.

Halibut is considered one of the most toothsome white-fleshed fish. If unavailable, halibut can be replaced in many recipes by tilefish, sea bass, or cod.

HERRING

Not too long ago herring were the most plentiful fish in the world's waters, but overfishing has taken its toll. This is a particularly worrisome development as herring are plankton converters and a source of food for many other species of fish, thus a crucial link in the ocean's ecosystem.

Americans are more familiar with herring that has been cured, such as pickled herring and kippered herring (also known as kippers), than they are with fresh herring, which is an oily fish with a distinctive flavor (reminiscent of mackerel) and a tender texture. In contrast, herring is a diet staple in Russia and much of Europe. Very small herring (2 to 3 inches in length) are sold as sardines. A limited quantity of sardines are sold fresh; most are salted, smoked, or canned.

Herring roe is appreciated in Japan, but until recently obtaining the roe meant sacrificing a great number of male fish to fertilizer or waste. This is because the process of "firming" the roe, which must take place before the roe can be removed from the female fish, renders the flesh inedible, and in the past the male fish were not separated before the firming began. Now, there are machines that can sort the fish by sex, which means the male fish never have to be subjected to the firming process and can be sold as fresh fillets instead.

KINGFISH

Kingfish is a common name for several species of drum (or croakers) found along the Atlantic Coast of the United States, all of which are small (rarely exceeding 12 inches), with lean, fine-textured white meat and good flavor. Though a member of the drum family, the kingfish does not have an air bladder and, therefore, cannot make the drumming noises for which the other members of this family are known.

If kingfish is unavailable, mackerel, bass, or mullet can be substituted in many recipes.

Kingfish is also a regional name for the king mackerel (found along the Atlantic Coast of the United States), a firm-textured fish that has a moderately strong flavor and is especially well suited for smoking.

If king mackerel is unavailable, tuna, swordfish, or amberjack can be substituted in many recipes.

LEMONFISH

Lemonfish, also known as cobia, cabio, ling, and crabeater, is the only member of its family. It is found in tropical temperate seas throughout the world, in the Western Atlantic from Cape Cod to Argentina, and in the Gulf of Mexico. It is a large fish, averaging between 30 and 50 pounds, though records indicate that specimens as large as 100 pounds have been caught.

The skin of lemonfish is very tough (and is usually removed before sale), but the meat is firm and white with large flakes. The flavor is very mild.

If lemonfish is unavailable, amberjack, snapper, grouper, or cod can be substituted in many recipes.

LOBSTER

European and American lobsters, both of which inhabit the North Atlantic, are the most famous members of the clawed lobster family. The American lobster, which is reddish brown with some brown spotting, lives in the western North Atlantic from Labrador to New Jersey and offshore as far south as North Carolina. The European lobster, which is bluish black with some yellowish white mottling, can be found in the North Sea, the Irish Sea, the English Channel, the Bay of Biscay, and in small numbers in the Mediterranean.

American lobsters, which make up 95 percent of the lobsters available in U.S. fisheries, can, if they are not caught, reach 50 pounds in weight and live up to 100 years. Common market size for American lobsters is about 1 to 2 pounds, which this animal reaches after 5 to 7 years and 20 to 30 molts (the shedding of its hard shell in order to grow a new, larger one). European lobsters are much smaller, growing to a maximum weight of about 8 pounds, but their market weight is similar to that of the American lobsters: between ¾ pound and 2 pounds.

Two delicious but less commercially significant kinds of lobsters available in the United States are clawless rock lobsters (also known as spiny lobsters), which are actually sea-dwelling crawfish, and small slipper lobsters (also known as Spanish, sand, shovel-nose, and locust lobsters).

MACKEREL

Mackerel is a very close relative of the tuna. Among the most well-known mackerels are Atlantic mackerel (also known as Boston mackerel), which is often used for sashimi and has more red meat than other mackerels; Pacific mackerel (also known as chub, blue, or American mackerel), which is tender and assertively flavored but most often canned; Spanish mackerel, which is leaner and more delicately flavored than other mackerels; and king mackerel, which has a very clean flavor. Also worth mentioning is wahoo, the gourmet member of the mackerel family, which is found in tropical and semitropical waters worldwide. In Hawaii it is called *ono*, meaning "good to eat." It is thought that "wahoo" is a corruption of the early European spelling of Oahu.

The soft, gray (sometimes pink) flesh of mackerel becomes off-white, firm, and flaky when cooked. The flavor can be more or less strong depending on the fish's oiliness, which varies not only with the species but also with the season.

Tuna, swordfish, or marlin can be substituted for mackerel in many recipes.

MAKO SHARK

Of the many species of shark, mako shark (also known as shortfin mako, sharp-nose shark, mackerel shark, and bonito shark) is considered among the best for eating. It is found in temperate and tropical waters in the Atlantic and Pacific oceans and can grow to a weight of 1,000 pounds in the space of five to six years. The off-white, moderately fatty meat, which is often compared to swordfish (and sometimes substituted for it), has a mild flavor, dense texture, and large flake. This fish never ceases swimming because it needs to swim in order to breathe.

If mako shark is unavailable, any meaty fish, such as catfish, tuna, swordfish, or marlin, can be substituted in many recipes.

MARLIN

The subject of Ernest Hemingway's *The Old Man and the Sea*, marlin have for a long time been a popular food fish in Japan (where they are used for sashimi and in sausage-making), Mexico, and Central and South America, but it is only recently that they have begun to show up on American tables. The marlin is a very large fish—it can weigh up to a ton—though the best meat comes from fish that weigh in at a svelte 150 pounds or less. Marlin is often compared to swordfish (because of its long bill). The flesh of marlin is lean and firm with large flakes and a moderately strong flavor.

If marlin is not available, swordfish or tuna can be substituted.

MONKFISH

Sort of like a monster with a heart of gold, the ugly-looking monkfish (also known as goosefish, frogfish, sea devil, bullmouth, bellyfish, and anglerfish) has surprisingly delicious meat; in fact, it is often compared to the meat of lobster. In Europe monkfish has long been prized, but in America fishermen threw this fish away until about fifteen years ago. Only the meat of the tail is used in the United States—the heads are usually discarded before they are even delivered to the fisheries—whereas in Europe the heads are simmered in stocks.

If monkfish is unavailable, grouper, tilefish, and lobster can be substituted in many recipes.

MULLET

Striped and silver mullet are the two most common species of mullet in markets in the U.S. This fish yields both light and dark meat and is quite popular in the South, where both the flesh and the roe are enjoyed. Most of the roe from mullet harvested in the United States, however, is shipped to Taiwan and the Middle East, where a high price is paid for its supposed powers as an aphrodisiac. The roe is also appreciated by the Japanese, who pan-sauté it for a dish called *karasumi*, and by the Italians, who press and salt it, then dry it in the sun, to make an antipasto dish called *bottarga*. The firm flesh has a rich, somewhat nutty flavor.

The red mullet, a superstar in the Mediterranean culinary world (where it is commonly cooked whole and ungutted), is not a mullet at all, but a member of the goatfish family.

MUSSELS

According to archaeological findings, mussels have been eaten for about 20,000 years, but modern-day Americans are just beginning to appreciate them. Europeans, on the other hand, especially the French, Dutch, and Spanish, are longtime devotees of this bivalve mollusk, which is known to have saved at least one life during the French Revolution. When the Minister of Justice gathered together a group of his colleagues to read a draft of the decree that would send Louis XVI to the guillotine, his cook was so appalled that she threw the paper to the floor and stomped on it. The minister's colleagues believed that the cook ought to be beheaded for this action, but after she prepared a mussel dish for them, they conceded to the minister that she was too good a cook to be sacrificed.

Throughout the world there are many species of mussels, their thin, oblong shells ranging in color from bright green to indigo blue to yellowish brown and their length ranging from 1½ to 6 inches. By far the most commonly available species in the United States is the blue mussel (also known as the edible or common mussel), which can be found clinging to rocks, sea walls, gravel, or any other surface that will support it, all along both the Atlantic and Pacific coasts. This mussel has a very dark blue shell that reaches 2 to 3 inches in length. Its ivory to bright orange meat has a slightly sweet flavor. In recent years the U.S. supply of these mussels has been greatly supplemented by cultured mussels, which have thinner, cleaner shells than wild mussels and also tend to be plumper and more uniform in size.

Of all shellfish, mussels are the most susceptible to pollution and pose the greatest risk of causing paralytic poisoning, an illness resulting from eating shellfish that have been contaminated by toxic blooms of algae known as red and brown tides. These days risk is minimized by vigilant monitoring of the shellfish supply, but as a precaution always shop at reputable fisheries and check with the local health department if gathering your own mussels, or any other kind of shellfish.

If mussels are unavailable, clams can be substituted in many recipes.

OCTOPUS

The octopus, a mollusk in the class Cephalopoda, is found in tropical and warm temperate seas worldwide. Though highly valued by people of many different countries, including China, Japan, Spain, Portugal, Italy, and Greece, Americans have had a hard time coming around to this eight-armed creature thought to be an aphrodisiac by the ancient Romans. Crabs, lobster, and abalone are among the standard diet of the octopus, so it is not surprising that its flesh is so flavorful. Contrary to popular opinion, the flesh of the octopus is not rubbery, as long as it is not overcooked.

If octopus is unavailable, squid can be substituted in many recipes.

OPAH

Opah, which is found throughout the Atlantic and Pacific oceans, is also known as moonfish because of its large, round profile. Its raw flesh is interestingly multi-colored—orangish behind the head and along the backbone, pinkish toward the belly, bright ruby red inside the breastplate, and dark red at the cheeks—but all of the flesh becomes white when cooked, except for the red part of the breast, which turns brown. This exotic fish's unique firm, coarse texture has earned it many new fans in recent years.

If opah is unavailable, tuna or pompano can be substituted in many recipes.

OYSTERS

Oyster cultivation, which began with the ancient Romans, takes place throughout the world, although the oyster population is way down because of waterfront de-velopment and pollution. There are two commercially important species of oys-ters in the United States: the Pacific (or Japanese) and the Atlantic (also known as Eastern or American). The oysters of each of these two species are given different names depending on where they are grown, for example, Wescott Bay and Willapa Bay on the Pacific Coast and Chincoteague, Chesapeake, and Blue Point on the East Coast. (The flavor and texture of oysters tend to vary depending on their environment—from bland to salty and soft to firm—and oyster connoisseurs swear by their favorites.) Pacific oysters, which can reach 12 inches in length, are considered inferior to Atlantic oysters. They were planted from Japanese seed in the 1920s. Atlantic oysters, which are smaller than Pacific oysters, are the tradi-tional half-shell oyster and make up the bulk of the U.S. oyster supply.

PIKE

Northern pike, also called common pike and pickerel, is found in the Great Lakes as well as in other large lakes in the northern United States and Canada, and is the only member of the pike family that is commercially significant. It has a silvery brown belly, a dark back, and light yellow spots on its side. The flesh, which is yellow when raw, is white, sweet, and breaks up easily when cooked. The top half of the fish holds tiny floating bones, which compels many cooks to avoid recipes that require filleting the fish and, instead, to use pike in recipes that call for puréed then strained fish, such as dumplings, mousses, and stuffings.

The French use pike to make dumplings called *quenelles de brochet.* It is also used in combination with whitefish and carp to make gefilte fish.

Walleye pike (also known as yellow pike) is not a pike at all but a perch.

If pike is unavailable, cod, orange roughy, or sole can be substituted in most recipes.

PLAICE

Plaice swim in the eastern North Atlantic, in the North Sea, around the British Isles, along the Norwegian coast, around Iceland and the Faroe Islands, and as far south and east as the coast of Sicily. The most important commercial flatfish in Europe, it belongs to the flounder family. As with all flatfish, after larval development, both eyes of the plaice move to one side of the head. (Most of the time the plaice's left eye joins the right eye on the right side of the head, though the reverse has been known to happen on occasion.) This movement of the eyes to one side of the head causes the body of the fish to tilt over until the left side of its body is facing the ocean floor. The plaice passes the rest of its life close to the ocean floor, swimming horizontally to it and looking up at the world. Its upper ("eyed") side is brown with reddish orange spots and there is a bony ridge between the eyes. The lower ("blind") side is white, as is the case with most flatfish.

Plaice flesh is white in color, fine in texture, and sweet in flavor.

If plaice is not available, most North American flounder or sole can be used instead.

POMPANO

Mark Twain said of pompano: "as delicious as the less criminal forms of sin." The pompano (also called sunfish) is found in subtropical waters from North Carolina to Florida, and is considered by many fish connoisseurs to be one of the finest fish available for eating, which is a great compliment to the fish but also keeps the price high for the consumer. Pompano does indeed boast a distinctive buttery taste and a firm yet delicate texture.

In Florida, where this fish is particularly abundant, it is commonly cooked with capers *en papillote* (wrapped in paper so the flavors and juices cannot escape). In Louisiana it is cooked *en papillote* as well, but the capers are replaced by a shrimp and crab meat sauce.

If pompano is unavailable, butterfish (also called California pompano) can often be substituted.

RED DRUM

Red drum (also known as channel bass, redfish, puppy drum, spottail bass, and red bass) is a member of the drum family and is found along the southeastern coast of the United States and in the Gulf of Mexico. The flesh of smaller red drum (weighing less than 10 pounds) is sweet and mild in flavor and flaky but moist in texture; the flesh of larger specimens tends to be coarse. Red drum have been the victims of overfishing and are, therefore, not as plentiful at the market as they used to be.

If red drum is unavailable, black drum, weakfish, or any other member of the drum family will make an acceptable substitute in many recipes.

RED MULLET

The red mullet, which is found in the Eastern Atlantic, the Bay of Biscay, the Mediterranean Sea, and the west coast of Africa to Senegal, is not a mullet at all, but belongs to the goatfish family. Like other goatfish, it has long chin barbels (used to locate food) that look like the whiskers on a goat. The mild white meat is firm and has few bones.

If red mullet is unavailable, sea bass or trout can be used instead.

SALMON

It is hard to imagine, given the popularity and price of salmon today, that in the eighteenth century indentured servants in the Colonies had it written into their contracts that they would not be served salmon more than once a week; farm workers in Brittany had no choice but to eat salmon three times a week; and servants in Norway were fed salmon five times a week.

Today the United States produces more salmon than any other country in the world, but it is by no means an inexpensive food that anyone would begrudge eating. It is a delicious fish worth preparing at home and ordering in restaurants.

There are six species available commercially—chinook, coho, sockeye, pink, and chum, which are native to the Pacific, and Atlantic salmon, the sole salmon native to the Atlantic Ocean—all of which are anadromous, which means they are born in fresh water, migrate to salt water to grow and mature, then return to fresh water to spawn. Pacific salmon die after they spawn once, whereas Atlantic salmon can repeat the migration and spawning cycle several times.

The Japanese are the largest consumers of Pacific salmon, eating it in many guises: raw, pickled, baked, salted, fried, smoked, and in soup. They also eat salmon livers, milt, and skulls, and process salmon into burgers and sausage.

Chinook salmon (also known as king, blackmouth, tyee, spring, and tullie) are the biggest of the Pacific salmon—the largest one on record weighed 126 pounds—but the more common market size is between 15 and 40 pounds. Chinook is a popular salmon for smoking.

Coho (also known as silver, silverside, and jack salmon) are known for the rich, reddish orange color of their meat (although some coho meat is pinkish), their excellent flavor, and large flake.

Most sockeye salmon (also known as red salmon and blueback) is either frozen for export or canned. Sockeye salmon is well liked by the Japanese, who appreciate the dark red color of the meat.

Pink salmon, also known as humpies because the males develop a hump on their backs when they reach sexual maturity, are considered the least valuable of salmon because they are not as oily or flavorful as the other species. They are the smallest salmon, averaging between 3 and 5 pounds, and the most plentiful. Much of the pink salmon catch is canned.

The best chum salmon, known as silverbrites, brites, or s. brites, are caught before they enter rivers to spawn. Most chum salmon (also known as dog, fall, and keta) is frozen or canned.

Fresh Atlantic salmon in U.S. markets, which is sometimes labeled according to its country of origin, such as Nova Scotia or Norway, is almost all farm-raised, as wild Atlantic salmon is a very rare commodity. Much of the Atlantic salmon catch is smoked.

Swordfish, tuna, trout, sole, or flounder can be substituted for salmon in many recipes.

SARDINES

The name "sardine" is applied to many small, young, soft-boned saltwater fish, such as Pacific and Atlantic herring, blueback herring, and sprat, as well as to true sardines, a Mediterranean species with which the sardine canning industry began on the island of Sardinia in the Mediterranean.

Fresh sardines, which have fatty flesh, are often grilled in Spain, Portugal, and France, but are hard to come by in the United States, where most people only know sardines in their canned form.

There is no substitute for fresh sardines.

SCALLOPS

Scallops, like clams and oysters, have two shells. They swim by snapping their shells together and, as a result of this swimming, develop an oversized muscle, called an "eye," which is the part of the scallop eaten by North Americans. Europeans differ in that they eat not only the muscle but also the flavorful pink roe that is attached to it. The flavor of scallops can be described as mildly sweet with nutlike overtones.

New England sea scallops, with muscles that can grow as large as 2 inches across, are the most widely available scallops in the United States. Scallop connoisseurs, however, seek out smaller and more tender bay scallops, whose muscles grow only to about ½ inch across. Another scallop that is becoming commercially significant is the calico scallop, a close relative of the bay scallop but slightly larger in size.

The color of scallops ranges from pale beige to creamy pink. Avoid scallops that are pure white because this is a sign that the scallops have been soaked in water, a technique that some manufacturers use to plump the scallops, jeopardizing the flavor in the process.

Though scallops get their name from their scalloped shells, it is uncommon to see a scallop in its shell at a fish market. This is because scallops are highly perishable and are usually shucked by fishermen right on board ship.

If scallops are unavailable, mussels can be substituted in many recipes.

SEA BREAM

Sea bream, also known as porgy, make up a large family of fish that swim in temperate and tropical waters worldwide. Most sea bream are lean and coarse-grained and have a delicate flavor. They also have a lot of small, sharp bones so it is best to buy the larger specimens because the meat-to-bone ratio is better, and the bones are easier to remove.

If sea bream is unavailable, red drum and amberjack can be used in many recipes.

SEA URCHIN

Though any bather who steps on a sea urchin will inevitably hold a grudge against this pincushion-like marine animal, anyone who has the opportunity to savor its cream- to orange-colored eggs will also inevitably seek them out again. These eggs, which are the only edible portion of the sea urchin, are in great demand in France, where they are often served on a slice of bread with a squirt of lemon, and in Japan, where they are eaten raw as sashimi or on a mound of white rice and are also made into a fermented sea urchin paste called *unishiokara*. There are hundreds of species of sea urchin roaming the Atlantic Ocean from Canada to the West Indies and the Pacific Ocean from Canada to Baja California.

If sea urchin is unavailable, oysters, mussels, or clams can be substituted in many recipes.

SHAD

Shad, which can weigh up to 14 pounds, is the largest member of the herring family. It is an anadromous fish, which means that it is born in fresh water, then migrates to the sea and stays there until it is ready to spawn, at which point it returns to its natal waters. Shad flesh has a delicate oiliness and a mildly sweet flavor reminiscent of pompano and salmon.

Sometimes called an inside-out porcupine, shad takes some skill to fillet. It can be purchased already filleted by the fishmonger or shad can be either steamed or baked whole at a low temperature for six hours or more so that the small bones disintegrate and the large backbone softens enough to become edible (making the filleting step completely unnecessary). Female shad are considered more desirable than male shad because they are larger and fatter (making them easier to fillet) and because they bear a valuable prize: their tasty roe.

If shad is unavailable, bluefish or Atlantic bonito can be used as a substitute in many recipes.

SHEEPSHEAD PORGY

Sheepshead porgy, a member of the porgy family that swims only in the Atlantic, does, in fact, boast a profile and teeth as well as browsing habits that can be said to resemble those of a sheep. It is also known as the convict fish, thanks to the dark stripes that adorn the sides of its body. Although it can grow as large as 20 pounds, it is usually caught before it reaches 15 pounds. Its flesh has a sweet flavor and a firm, flaky taste.

At the beginning of the nineteenth century, sheepshead porgy swam in great abundance around Long Island—Sheepshead Bay in Brooklyn was named after this fish—but it is no longer found in that area because the water has gotten too cold and the sheepshead have moved south.

Sheepshead porgy is no relation to the California sheepshead, which swims in the Pacific Ocean, or the freshwater drum, which swims mainly in large rivers and lakes and is commonly known as sheepshead.

If sheepshead porgy is not available, any member of the drum family, especially black drum or tilefish, can be used as a substitute.

SHRIMP

There are hundreds of species of shrimp throughout the world; in fact, shrimp is the most widely consumed of all seafood. In the United States shrimp can be found off the coast of Maine and from South Carolina to the Gulf of Mexico. They are also imported from India, Bangladesh, Thailand, and many of the Central and South American countries. In general, the medium- to large-sized shrimp, often sold unpeeled and uncooked in our markets, are from warm waters while the tiny pink shrimp, commonly sold peeled and cooked, are from cold waters.

The heads of shrimp are full of wonderful flavors, but shrimp that have not had their heads removed are difficult to find in the United States. (The American fish industry prefers to remove the heads because whole shrimp spoil more quickly than headless shrimp.) For the recipes in this book—and any other time shrimp is on your menu—try to find shrimp with heads on either in a fish market in an Asian community or in any other very high-quality fish market.

There is much confusion regarding the different uses of the words "shrimp" and "prawn." According to A. J. McClane, one of this country's most highly regarded fish experts, all freshwater species of this crustacean are prawns and all marine species are shrimp.

In usage, however, the differences are not so clear. In the United States, "prawn" is often used to describe large or "jumbo" shrimp (those that count fifteen or fewer to the pound). In England, however, very small canned shrimp are called shrimp and all other larger shrimp are deemed prawns. To add to the confusion, what many people call Dublin Bay prawns (also known as langoustines) are not prawns at all but a kind of miniature lobster. In Italy, however, Dublin Bay prawns are known as scampi. The dish shrimp scampi (shrimp sautéed with butter and garlic) is purely American and not even known in Italy.

SKATE

Skate, which is considered a delicacy in Europe, has recently started to gain popularity in the United States. It is a member of the ray family and a cousin to the shark, and is found in the Atlantic and Pacific as well as in other temperate waters throughout the world. It has a broad, flat body; triangular "wings" (actually enlarged pectoral fins) that jut out from both sides of its body; and a long, thin tail. The "wings," which are divided by cartilage, provide the boneless edible portion of the fish, which is sweet, mild, and somewhat gelatinous.

If skate is unavailable, catfish, shark, or sturgeon can be used as a substitute in many recipes.

SOLE

Of the five species of true sole that roam the U.S. Atlantic, none are good eating fish. There are numerous North American flounders, such as petrale sole, lemon sole, rex sole, and butter sole, that are sold under the name "sole," but none of them are actually members of the sole family. True sole, the best known of which is Dover sole (also known as Channel, European, or black sole), come from Europe. Dover sole is eagerly sought out for its delicate flavor and firm texture. Thickback sole (also known as bastard sole and variegated sole) and lascar (also known as French sole and sand sole), two other true soles, are occasionally available in American markets, but neither is as highly esteemed as Dover sole.

If sole is unavailable, flounder, plaice, or whitefish can be substituted in many recipes.

SQUID

Squid (also known as calamari) is a relative of both the octopus and the cuttlefish. It is especially popular among Mediterranean, Oriental, and Mexican cooks and is gaining popularity in the United States.

There are three main species of the ten-armed cephalopod harvested in this country: the long-finned (or winter) squid and the short-finned (or summer) squid from the East Coast, and the opalescent squid (also known as California or Monterey squid) from the West Coast. The long-fin and opalescent are usually more tender than the short-fin. Giant squid (about 5 pounds) are imported from Argentina, Mexico, and Japan and sold as pretenderized steaks, sometimes under the name "grande calamari steaks."

Cleaning squid can be difficult for the squeamish or hurried so if you are either or both, have your fishmonger do it for you. When cooked properly—1 to 2 minutes per side is usually enough—squid is slightly sweet and firm yet tender, but if overcooked it can be tough. The remedy for overcooked squid is actually more cooking; after about 20 minutes total cooking time squid becomes tender again.

If squid is unavailable, octopus can be substituted in many recipes.

STRIPED BASS

Striped bass (also known as rockfish and striper) is in a sense to be thanked for the American public school system, at least the beginnings of it. In 1670 in the Plymouth Colony it was ordered that all income that the Cape Cod fisheries earned from the sale of bass, mackerel, and herring be used to fund a free school, and it was mainly through the sale of striped bass that the doors of the New World's first school were opened.

Unfortunately, striped bass, a saltwater fish that goes to freshwater to reproduce, is not nearly so bountiful today. In fact, due to overfishing and pollution in rivers where the young hatch, the availability of striped bass for eating has become limited in many areas. Though they can grow up to 125 pounds, striped bass are better for eating when they are much smaller—less than 12 pounds. The meat has a mild flavor, soft texture, and large flake.

If striped bass is unavailable, trout can be used instead in many recipes.

STURGEON

Sturgeon are the source of caviar, the most valuable fish roe in the world. Not surprisingly, after years of overfishing in order to obtain this roe, sturgeon started to become extremely scarce; fortunately, strict fishing limitations have been enacted and farming has begun to take up some of the slack. Though perhaps not quite as famous as the roe, the flesh of the sturgeon is sought after in both its fresh and smoked forms. Fresh sturgeon meat is very firm and delicately flavored.

If sturgeon is unavailable, shark or catfish can often be substituted.

SWORDFISH

The swordfish gets its name from its flat swordlike upper jaw and snout, which can account for up to one third of its length. This ever-popular fish lives in warm and tropical waters throughout the world. In the United States it is caught off the coasts of California, New England, and Florida and in the Gulf of Mexico. In addition, in the past few years new swordfish grounds have been found northwest of the Hawaiian Islands around Midway Island, and companies in Honolulu ship these fish to some of America's major metropolitan cities. The demand for swordfish is so great, however, that additional fish are being imported from such places as Chile, Brazil, Spain, Portugal, and even Greece.

Swordfish can weigh as much as 1,000 pounds but are usually caught before they reach 250 pounds. In the past fishermen would land swordfish by driving harpoons into their backs but today fishermen more commonly use long lines fitted with thousands of hooks.

The uncooked meat of swordfish may be orange, pink, or white, but it all turns the same light color when cooked and it all tastes equally good and boasts the same steaklike quality.

If swordfish is unavailable, shark, tuna, and salmon can generally be substituted.

TILAPIA

The tilapia, a fish native to Africa, was introduced into rivers in the United States in the late 1960s to control algae. It is a highly adaptable fish that can survive almost anywhere, and high-quality farmed hybrids are becoming available in more significant quantities. Good tilapia is lean, moist, tender, and mild-tasting, but quality can vary so be sure to buy it from a reputable fishmonger.

If tilapia is unavailable, flounder can often be substituted.

TILEFISH

Tilefish, which feed on crabs, shrimp, squid, and mollusks, live in tropical and temperate waters worldwide and range in size from 20 to 50 pounds. The flavor of their firm, white flesh is often described as a cross between lobster and codfish.

In 1882, due to what is now believed to have been an influx of cold water, virtually the entire tilefish population was extinguished, leaving 4,250 square miles of the Atlantic covered with dead tilefish. Slowly the population began to reappear and in the 1970s the tilefish landing in Barnegat Light, New Jersey, was so high that this small town became known as the "tilefish capital of the world." Today tilefish is most popular in major metropolitan areas, and is winning over new fans elsewhere every day.

If tilefish is unavailable, drum can be substituted in many recipes.

TROUT (BROWN AND RAINBOW)

Trout are found in waters throughout the world, but all the trout in American markets are farm raised. Rainbow trout, which owes its name to a reddish pink band that often stretches from its gillcover practically to its tail, is the most popular trout in American markets. Brown trout, also known as sea trout and salmon trout, is much more widely marketed in Europe than in the United States. Both brown and rainbow trout are mildly flavored, small flaked, and firm.

If trout is unavailable, salmon can be substituted in many recipes.

TUNA

Given its amazing meatlike flavor and texture, it is hard to believe that until recently Americans knew tuna only as a canned product. On the other hand, the Japanese—the world's biggest consumers of tuna in fresh and frozen form—have long appreciated this unique fish and, in fact, they send seafood buyers to the United States to buy some of the best specimens for Tokyo's Tsukiji Market. Of the thirteen species of tuna, the best ones for eating are bluefin, bigeye, yellowfin, Atlantic bonito, and blackfin.

The bluefin tuna, which swims in temperate and subtropical waters worldwide, gets its name from its steel blue color. This is the largest tuna—it has the potential to tip the scales at 1,500 pounds but usually arrives at U.S. markets at about 150 pounds.

Bigeye tuna, which has unusually large eyes, swims in the Atlantic, Pacific, and Indian oceans. This tuna, which generally arrives at the market at about 100 pounds (though it has been known to reach 500 pounds), is considered the second-best tuna for sashimi following bluefin.

Yellowfin tuna is so named because of its long, bright yellow fins and the stripe of yellow on its side. The most commonly available tuna in the United States, it can reach a weight of 350 pounds in as few as seven years but usually arrives at markets at 100 pounds or less. Yellowfin tuna live in warm temperate waters worldwide.

Atlantic bonito is found in the Atlantic Ocean as well as the Mediterranean and Black seas. It is a small tuna, averaging about 25 pounds, and has a stronger flavor than the other tuna listed here. Do not confuse Atlantic bonito with little tunny, which is sometimes referred to as bonito in the South but is of lesser quality.

Blackfin is found in the Western Atlantic from Cape Cod to Brazil. It usually weighs under 20 pounds at market but can reach about 60 pounds in the sea. It is also popular for sashimi. This fish is of excellent quality, but is not easy to come by in American markets.

TURBOT

Turbot, a European flatfish appreciated for its delicate flavor and firm white flesh, is usually imported into the United States frozen. This fish can reach 30 pounds but usually weighs in at the market at about 3 to 6 pounds.

If turbot is unavailable, halibut, brill, flounder, or weakfish can be substituted in many recipes.

WEAKFISH

Weakfish, part of the drum (or croaker) family, is so named because of its delicate mouth structure, which can be torn easily by a hook. It also goes by the names sea trout, speckled trout, gray sea trout, squeteague, and summer trout. Its flesh is white, sweet, lean, and finely textured. This fish can reach 8 pounds but is usually caught when it still weighs between 3 and 7 pounds.

If weakfish is unavailable, striped bass, trout, salmon, or any member of the drum family can be substituted in many recipes.

WHITEBAIT

The term "whitebait" refers not to a single fish, but to the young of a variety of species, including herring, smelts, silversides, sand lances, and anchovies, served whole and ungutted. To be considered whitebait, a fish cannot measure more than 2½ inches. Whitebait tends to have moderately strong flavor and a soft, fine-flaked texture.

Baby herring and its kin are commonly sold as whitebait in Europe; very young silversides or sand lances are popular in the States.

WHITING

Whiting (sometimes referred to as European whiting) is the name for a European fish reminiscent of cod. Whiting is also a common name for an American fish known by the names New England hake, frostfish, and silver hake (because the fish has a silvery, iridescent sheen when pulled from the water). This fish is mild with small flakes.

Hoki, a related species found in large quantities off the coast of New Zealand and sold throughout the United States, hake, or cod may be used in many recipes that call for whiting.

BUTTER

Some confusion may arise over the measuring of butter and other hard fats. In the United States, butter is generally sold in one-pound packages that contain four equal "sticks." The wrapper on each stick is marked to show tablespoons, so the cook can cut the stick according to the quantity required. The equivalent weights are:

   1 stick = 115 g/4 oz

   1 tablespoon = 15 g/½ oz

FLOUR

American all-purpose flour is milled from a mixture of hard and soft wheats, whereas British plain flour is made mainly from soft wheat. To achieve a near equivalent to American all-purpose flour, use half British plain flour and half strong bread flour.

SUGAR

In the recipes in this book, if sugar is called for it is assumed to be granulated, unless otherwise specified. American granulated sugar is finer than British granulated, closer to caster sugar, so British cooks should use caster sugar throughout.

INGREDIENTS AND EQUIPMENT GLOSSARY

British English and American English are not always the same, particularly in the kitchen. The following ingredients and equipment are basically the same on both sides of the Atlantic, but have different names.

AMERICAN	BRITISH
arugula	rocket
baking soda	bicarbonate of soda
beans (dried)—lima, navy, Great Northern	dried white (haricot) beans
Belgian endive	chicory
bell pepper	sweet pepper (capsicum)
Bibb and Boston lettuce	soft-leaved, round lettuce
broiler/to broil	grill/to grill
cheesecloth	muslin
chile	chilli
cornstarch	cornflour
crushed hot red pepper	dried crushed red chilli
eggplant	aubergine
heavy cream (37.6% fat)	whipping cream (35–40% fat)
hot pepper sauce	Tabasco sauce
kitchen towel	tea towel
lowfat milk	semi-skimmed milk
parchment paper	nonstick baking paper
peanut oil	groundnut oil
pearl onion	button or baby onion
romaine lettuce	cos lettuce
Romano cheese	pecorino cheese
scallion	spring onion
shrimp	prawn (varying in size)
skillet	frying pan
tomato purée	sieved tomatoes or pasatta
whole milk	homogenized milk
zucchini	courgette

VOLUME EQUIVALENTS

These are not exact equivalents for the American cups and spoons, but have been rounded up or down slightly to make measuring easier.

AMERICAN MEASURES	METRIC	IMPERIAL
¼ t	1.25 ml	
½ t	2.5 ml	
1 t	5 ml	
½ T (1½ t)	7.5 ml	
1 T (3 t)	15 ml	
¼ cup (4 T)	60 ml	2 fl oz
⅓ cup (5 T)	75 ml	2½ fl oz
½ cup (8 T)	125 ml	4 fl oz
⅔ cup (10 T)	150 ml	5 fl oz (¼ pint)
¾ cup (12 T)	175 ml	6 fl oz
1 cup (16 T)	250 ml	8 fl oz
1¼ cups	300 ml	10 fl oz (½ pint)
1½ cups	350 ml	12 fl oz
1 pint (2 cups)	500 ml	16 fl oz
1 quart (4 cups)	1 litre	1¾ pints

OVEN TEMPERATURES

In the recipes in this book, only Fahrenheit temperatures have been given. Consult this chart for the Centigrade and gas mark equivalents.

OVEN	°F	°C	GAS MARK
very cool	250–275	130–140	½–1
cool	300	150	2
warm	325	170	3
moderate	350	180	4
moderately hot	375	190	5
	400	200	6
hot	425	220	7
very hot	450	230	8
	475	250	9

WEIGHT EQUIVALENTS

The metric weights given in this chart are not exact equivalents, but have been rounded up or down slightly to make measuring easier.

AVOIRDUPOIS	METRIC
¼ oz	7 g
½ oz	15 g
1 oz	30 g
2 oz	60 g
3 oz	90 g
4 oz	115 g
5 oz	150 g
6 oz	175 g
7 oz	200 g
8 oz (½ lb)	225 g
9 oz	250 g
10 oz	300 g
11 oz	325 g
12 oz	350 g
13 oz	375 g
14 oz	400 g
15 oz	425 g
1 lb	450 g
1 lb 2 oz	500 g
1½ lb	750 g
2 lb	900 g
2¼ lb	1 kg
3 lb	1.4 kg
4 lb	1.8 kg
4½ lb	2 kg

As with most projects of this scope, the creation of this book has been very much a team effort rather than the concentrated work of one person. I would particularly like to thank the people at Northwest Airlines, especially Gary Franson; the cooks and staff of the Windsor Court Hotel; writer Terri Landry; photographer Louis Wallach; book designer Jim Wageman; project editor Melanie Falick; and Stewart, Tabori & Chang publisher Leslie Stoker.

I would also like to express my gratitude to those New Orleans businesses and individuals who so generously contributed many of the props and locations for the photographs. They include Les Kubans; Dansk; Patout Antiques; Dozier Antiques; Casy Willems Pottery; Lucullus Culinary Antiques, Art and Objects; Diane Genke Oriental Art and Antiques; Shady Side Pottery of New Orleans; Judy: A Gallery of Decorative Arts; Animal Art Antiques; Glenn Vesh of Perfect Presentations; Steve and Milton; Betty Norris; and the San Francisco Plantation House in Reserve, Louisiana.

Finally, a special note of appreciation goes to Mr. and Mrs. James Coleman, Sr., for their continuing support of my work.

Designed by Jim Wageman

Composed with QuarkXpress 3.1 on a Macintosh IIsi in Centaur and Gill Sans
by Barbara Sturman at Stewart, Tabori & Chang, New York.
Output on a Linotronic L300 at Typogram, New York, New York.

Printed and bound by
Toppan Printing Company, Ltd.,
Tokyo, Japan.